UNTIL FURTH

Until Further Notice...

Theresienstadt On My Mind

UNTIL FURTHER NOTICE...: THERESIENSTADT ON MY MIND
Copyright © 2024

KTAV PUBLISHING HOUSE
527 Empire Blvd
Brooklyn, NY 11225
www.ktav.com
orders@ktav.com

Ph: (718) 972-5449 / Fax: (718) 972-6307

ISBN 978-1-60280-507-1

Set in Arno Pro by Raphaël Freeman MISTD, Renana Typesetting

History will justify anything. It teaches precisely nothing for it contains everything and furnishes examples of everything. History is the most dangerous product evolved from the chemistry of the intellect. — Paul Valéry

In memory of my parents

November 1, 1939. The only surviving prewar photograph of my parents,
Barend Boas and Anna de Haas. The bridesmaids Anna Papegaai
and Anna Soes reached the age of six and thirteen years, respectively.

Acknowledgments

Historians rely on multiple agencies, human and otherwise. As to the former, first and foremost my wife, Patricia, for her unstinting support and advice. I am grateful to Ann Haroun for offering useful input on practically every aspect, from grammar to documentation. I owe a special debt of gratitude to Brent Gregston, whose editing skills improved the manuscript substantially. Honorable mentions and more: Camp Westerbork Researcher Bas Kortholt; Christa Stevens; Lower Saxony/Osnabrück archivist Thomas Brakmann; Willa Schneberg; Yoka Verdoner; Laureen Nussbaum; Karen Weliky; Ger Landa. Then there are the unsung, behind-the-scenes heroes, archivists and programmers securing access to the indispensable documents of the trade. To all, many, many thanks.

Contents

Introduction

After being helped with his coat, hat, and gloves by a subordinate he has summoned with a bell, Commandant leaves office to go on inspection tour of the camp.

– From the film script of Westerbork

The book's title, *Until Further Notice*... refers to exemptions that temporarily shielded Holland's Jews from deportation, a holding pattern that invariably came to grief against the iron law of the "Final Solution," for every exemption carried an expiration date forebodingly framed as *bis auf weiteres* (until further notice). The principal conduit for making Holland Judenfrei – "Jew-free" – was Westerbork, the transit camp located in the northeastern part of the country from which 105,000 Dutch Jews and several hundred Sinti and Roma were dispatched to the killing centers in Poland. The camp was liberated by Canadian troops in April 1945.

The subtitle, *Theresienstadt On My Mind*, alludes to the Holocaust and my fate under the Ostuf, i.e., camp commandant Obersturmbahnführer Albert Konrad Gemmeker. The Ostuf took a personal interest in my family's wellbeing, signing off on our deportation to Theresienstadt (Terezín in Czech), the so-called *Musterlager* (Model Camp) in the German Protectorate of Bohemia and Moravia. In the Nazi optic, this was a perk reserved for the "lucky" few and the best anyone at Westerbork could hope for. In Nazi parlance, deportation to Theresienstadt amounted to no more than *Wohnsitzverlegung*: "change of residence."

The card registering our prospective deportation to the *Musterlager*

```
                 Fortsetzung.

Bo ns           Barend              11.9.18
-----------------------------------------------

24.12.43.Meldung Antragstelle:Sperrung
wegen Schwangerschaft der Frau aufgehobe
da Kind am 1.11.43 geboren.

2o.1.44. Zurueckgestellt durch
    Weinrebliste I

    3.2.44.Weinreb-Sperre aufgehoben.

10.2.44 Kind Marcus a.d. Krhs. entl.

10.2.44 Frau Anna a.d.Krhs. entl.

10.2.44 Kind Jacob a.d.Krhs. entl.

6.3.44.Meldung Antragstelle: Mann,bezw.
Vater arbeitet beim Aussenkommando den
Haag(Rueckstellung Ed.)xxx

12.3.44 Sind laut Anordn. Ostuf. fuer
Theresienstadt vorgesehen. Meldung
Antragstelle.
```

was made out in my father's name, Barend Boas (9/11, 1918). The first item below the dotted line states that on December 12, 1943, our exemption (*Sperrung*) related to my mother's pregnancy had been terminated by virtue of my entry into the world in the early morning of November 1: inmate 8331. For an odd – not say, sadistic – twist in Westerbork's *Gestalt* was that women in their third trimester of pregnancy were not to be deported until six weeks after giving birth, together with the newborn and the rest of the family. *Frau Anna's* "maternity leave," framed as a humanitarian gesture, was of a piece with other tokens of goodwill (sporting events, chess tournaments, cabarets, concerts, and the like) calculated to foster the illusion that similar conditions might well prevail in the alleged "work camps in the

East," ensuring a well-nigh frictionless deportation regimen. Shades of Theresienstadt. And, as in Theresienstadt, there was a film purporting to show that conditions were tolerable, if not downright pleasant.[1]

Indeed, for those who succeeded in prolonging their stay in Westerbork the camp was not intolerable. Within its perimeter was relief from the German persecution in the rest of Holland. In the transit camp, from the policeman up to the chief administrator, Jews were in authority. Even so, the atmosphere was rife with the human grating of nerves stretched by the will to live. The name inmates gave to the road that ran alongside the railway platform captured the camp's essence to a T: Boulevard des Misères.

On January 20, 1944, Westerbork's *Antragstelle*, the camp's Application Office tasked with processing requests for exemptions, recorded that we had been exempted once more, this time through "Weinreb Liste I," the brainchild of a Jewish conman guaranteeing those on it an unobstructed passage to South America (see chapters V and VI). This exemption lasted until February 3. The card further indicates that

---

1. The Westerbork film, made in the spring 1944 by order of commandant Gemmeker, was intended to convey the impression that the camp was being run by an enlightened despot. The exception was the "transport scene," a staple in every documentary about the Holocaust – included, the commandant declared at his postwar trial in the Netherlands, to show the "sadder aspects, in order that it might not be said that I only focused on the better side of the camp." Jacob Boas, *Boulevard des Misères: The Story of Transit Camp Westerbork* (Hamden Connecticut, Archon Books, 1985), 31. The film was directed by German Jewish refugee Rudolf Breslauer. Breslauer was deported to Auschwitz in 1944 and murdered. https://www.youtube.com/watch?v=8E-IWGjbGZM and https://www.niod.nl/en/news/westerborkfilm-exhibition. The propaganda film about Theresienstadt, "The Führer Gives a City to the Jews," filmed for the most part in the fall of 1944, was directed by Kurt Gerron. Gerron played Brown in the *Three Penny Opera* and the magician opposite Marlene Dietrich in the film *The Blue Angel*. Gerron entered the Netherlands in 1933 and, like Breslauer, was eventually interned in Westerbork. The surviving twenty minutes of footage depicted Jews checking books out of the library, swimming, gardening, playing cards, attending a football match and concerts, etc., among other leisurely pursuits. Upon completion of the film, Gerron was deported to Auschwitz and murdered. https://www.youtube.com/watch?v=P9V6d2Y1WjE..

on February 10, my mother, brother Max, and I had been released from the camp hospital (respectively, jaundice, polio, pneumonia). On March 6, the Applications Office confirmed that my father *arbeitet beim Aussenkommdo den Haag* – "works at external command in The Hague" – at the behest, no less, of the "BdS," *Befehlshaber der Sicherheitsdienst* (Commander of the Security Police). Six days later, the commandant put us down for Theresienstadt. Up till then, Barend had worked in Westerbork's tailoring workshop. Farmed out to German headquarters in The Hague, he spent the better part of a year putting the *Über* in the *Übermensch*, sewing uniforms and leisure suits fit for the Master Race. I can only surmise that the order to pack us off to the "Ghetto Paradise" came from higher ups: a "Model Camp" deserved a "Model Tailor."

This was how we managed to stave off deportation "to the East" – and death. For there can be no doubt whatsoever that for us – a family of four including two children with a combined age of 4.5 – Theresienstadt was just another waystation on track to the Auschwitz gas chamber. Hence "on my mind." Here I might add, parenthetically, that over and above a temporary stay of execution, "until further notice" is embedded in historiography in the guise of revisionism. The Dutch historian Pieter Geyl described his discipline as a "debate without end." Several chapters in the ensuing work bear him out.

Since we never left Holland, Theresienstadt is not "on my mind" in the sense of having any memories of it. Nor do I of Westerbork. Yet the fact of being born in the transit camp has struck deep, impenetrable roots within me, coupled with a seemingly unslakable need to "know." In vain. I am like Kafka's man in *The Trial* who fails to get admittance to the Law. "The doorkeeper sees that the man is nearing his end, and in order to reach his failing hearing, he roars at him: 'No one else could gain admittance here, because this entrance was meant solely for you. I am going to go and shut it now.'"[2]

And yet I wait.

---

2. *The Trial*, trans. Breon Mitchell (New York: Random House, 1998), 215–16.

Set for the most part in the Netherlands, the book's overarching theme, spread out over six interrelated, amplifying chapters, is the precarity of decision-making in the face of war, occupation, and persecution – a volatile mix rife with the spirit of *J'Accuse*. In each chapter, choice, the preeminence of an individual's conduct, however delimited under the circumstances, is present in one form or another. The fact, for example, that Himmler had to talk his SS-minions into staying the course in the mass slaughter of Jews shows that even among the utterly dehumanized and brutalized there were those who balked. The men and women of the White Rose said NO and paid for it with their lives. In Transit Camp Westerbork an elderly German-Jewish writer rejects a potentially life-saving Paraguayan passport. A Jewish woman is caught with a fake identity card on a railway platform, deported to Sobibor, and murdered. In the Netherlands, the decision as to who was and wasn't Jewish lay with a Nazi-appointed "Race Consultant." Jews had to decide whether to register as Jews, go into hiding (provided they had the means and requisite contacts), flee the country, or, as a parent, give up a child, often to total strangers, in the hope of saving it (my parents refused such an offer for their then only child, Max).

Dutch office holders and public servants had to decide whether to play ball with the occupier, or resign. In the Netherlands as in Germany, writers, publishers, artists, actors, and entertainers risked marginalization unless they joined a Nazified Cultural Chamber. Others again, risked imprisonment, or worse, for sheltering and hiding Jews. Confronted with a seemingly endless occupation, the vast majority chose to keep a low profile and noses clean.

The Netherlands was invaded in May of 1940, breaching the country's neutrality. The Queen and her government fled to England on the 13th, Holland capitulated two days later. After a brief period of military rule, Hitler installed a civilian government headed by Reichkommissar Arthur Syess-Inquart, the Austrian politician who earned his spurs steering his country into the German orbit. Unlike in neighboring Belgium, where military rule prevailed, in Holland the SS called the shots, with all-around fatal consequences.

Victorious, the occupier took its time applying the screws. In the first year, Jews were dismissed from the Dutch press, forbidden to practice ritual slaughter, and barred from joining their non-Jewish neighbors in civil defense maneuvers – the overture to a whirlwind of decrees that kept Jews in a permanent state of tension and wracked with fear. Anne Frank, June 20, 1942:

> Anti-Jewish decrees followed each other in quick succession. Jews must wear a yellow star. Jews must hand in their bicycles. Jews are banned from trams and are forbidden to drive, Jews are only allowed to do their shopping between three and five o'clock and then only in shops which bear the sign "Jewish shops." Jews must be indoors by eight o'clock and cannot even sit in their own gardens

after that hour. Jews are forbidden to visit theaters, cinemas and other places of entertainment. Jews may not take part in public sports...Jews may not visit Christians. Jews must go to Jewish schools, and many more such restrictions of a similar kind.

Anne Frank's diary helped create, and perpetuate, the myth of the Dutch standing shoulder to shoulder with their Jewish compatriots in the unfolding catastrophe. History tells a different story. Proportionally more Jews were deported from Holland than from any other Western European country: 105,000 of 140,000 – 75%. A mere five thousand survived. Hannah Arendt called the destruction of Dutch Jewry "a disaster unparalleled in any Western country." This is "Holland's paradox."[3] The contradiction of a country where antisemitism was low-key and Jews, 1.5 percent of the population in 1940, had been thoroughly integrated before being killed on a mass scale second only to Polish Jewry.

While it is true that many thousands risked their lives to help Jews – 28,000 Jews in hiding were saved[4] – and in February 1941 workers in Amsterdam struck in sympathy with Jews, it is also true that the Dutch banks, insurance companies, the railway, the civil service, the regular police and the policemen of the Dutch SS, worked in tandem to expropriate, collect and transport the Jewish citizens to death camps.

In 2020, Netherlands' Prime Minister Mark Rutte officially acknowledged the state's failing as "guardians of morality and security" at the nation's Holocaust commemoration. "Too many functionaries carried out the occupier's dictates," he added. "The bitter consequences of the registration and deportation were not recognized in time. Now that the last of the survivors are among us, I today offer my apologies."[5]

---

3. Peter Romijn, *Der lange Krieg der Niederlande: Besatzung, Gewalt und Neuorientierung in den vierziger Jahren* (Göttingen: Wallstein Verlag, 2017), 107.
4. Ibid., 108.
5. Cited in Wim de Wagt, *Vijfhonderd meter namen: De Holocaust en de pijn van de herinnering* (Five-hundred-meter names: The Holocaust and the pain of the memory) (Amsterdam: Boom, 2021), 179.

The government in exile in London was no better. Its (illegal) broadcasts to the Netherlands rarely mentioned the death camps in Poland nor alerted the Jewish Council, the instrument installed by the occupier in late February 1941 to help implement its anti-Jewish policies. Though information was sketchy, there was enough to sound the alarm. "The English radio [BBC] speaks of their [Jews] being gassed," wrote Anne Frank in October 1942.

The final year of the occupation was especially rough. In 1944, the occupier called up thousands of men to work in Germany, triggering a short-lived railway strike. Germany cut off coal and food supplies. The ensuing winter, the so-called Hunger Winter, claimed 20,000 lives. Stepped up brutality begot stepped-up resistance. The end of the war left Holland exhausted and traumatized – and bereft of three quarters of its prewar Jewish population.

Judgment is intrinsic to doing history. It cannot be avoided no matter how conscientiously and rigorously pursued. Truth, impartiality, justice are variable properties. As a rule, the discipline teaches us to reserve judgment and leave it to the future to judge. Historians decide what to cover and what to leave out, in short, exercising judgment. *Until Further Notice...* cites two historians with contrasting views on this head: French medievalist Marc Bloch and Dutch Jewish historian Jacques (Jacob) Presser (see Chapters IV and VI). Bloch cautioned historians against injecting judgments; Presser's magnum opus, *The Destruction of Dutch Jews*, bristled with aggrieved victimhood and finger-pointing; he wrote it, he said, "with blood."[6]

Translations are mine, unless noted.

*   *   *

---

6. Philo Bregstein, *Gesprekken met Jacques Presser* (Conversations with Jacques Presser) (Amsterdam: Polak & Van Gennep Uitgeversmaatschappij NV, 1971), 118.

Chapter I
Beware of Pity

Pity: a feeling of sadness or sympathy for the suffering or unhappiness of others.   – Merriam-Webster

Henri has discovered that pity, being a primary and instinctive sentiment, grows quite well if ably cultivated, particularly in the primitive minds of the brutes who command us, those very brutes who have no scruples about beating us up without a reason, or treading our faces into the ground.   – Primo Levi

Among other vices, I cruelly hate cruelty, both by nature and by judgment, as the extreme of all vices.   – Montaigne

1. Jud Süss, the Eternal Jew

Jud Süss (1940), a venomous Jew-bashing clicherama masquerading as entertainment, premiered in Germany in September 1940. Perversely based on the eponymous novel by the German-Jewish author Lion Feuchtwanger, the film's setting is the eighteenth-century Duchy of Württemberg and its capital Stuttgart, a land of milk and honey governed by a profligate, lecherous duke. When the spigot to fund his pet projects – personal bodyguard, opera, and ballet company – is turned off, Duke Karl Alexander turns to Joseph Süss Oppenheimer, a wealthy Frankfurt Jew, to pick up the tab. Süss shaves his beard, cuts his hair, dons "Christian" garb, pockets the pass from the duke giving him unimpeded entry to Stuttgart (Jews were banned from Württemberg's capital), licks his chops, and off he goes, posthaste. The roads are in terrible shape and no match for the speeding bankroller. Süss' carriage flies off the road and lands in a ditch. Stranded, he hitches a ride with Dorothea, a blonde maiden of the purest Aryan stock, the archetype of the clueless *Fräulein* taken in by the wily Jew; the twosome enter Stuttgart without a hitch. Jud Süss underwrites the duke's projects and showers him with jewels, the better to seduce the ladies. Having extracted sole authority to levy tolls on roads and bridges, Süss bleeds the duchy dry and succeeds in having the ban on Jews lifted.

Left to their own devices, the latter go on the rampage. Süss rapes Dorothea; tortures both her father and the girl's fiancé, Faber; Dorothea drowns herself; the duke succumbs to a heart attack. With the Duchy about to go to seed, Faber's Aryan DNA saves the day. Süss, tried for "having carnal knowledge of a Christian woman," is hanged on the gallows. *Jud Süss* ends with a warning to take the film's message to heart, from generation to generation.

The recipient of the Golden Lion award at (Mussolini's) 1940 Venice Film Festival, the film was a smash hit. No expense was spared to bring this cautionary tale to the public and Nazi cohorts at home and abroad. In its first year alone, one out of every three Germans paid to see it. Moshe Flinker, a sixteen-year-old Dutch Jewish boy who saw the film in Brussels, where he lived as a foreigner under an assumed name, was appalled. The film made his "blood boil." "I was red in the face when I came out," Moshe wrote in his diary. "In the film, a Jew is made to say: 'We, too, have a God, but this God is the God of Vengeance.' This is a lie, pure and simple. Our Lord is the same Lord who said, 'Love thy neighbor as thyself,' but now I pray He may appear as the Lord of Vengeance."[1]

It is unlikely that German moviegoers left the theater feeling sorry for Jud Süss Oppenheimer as they might for the Jews vilified in *The Eternal Jew*, a one-hour and five-minute shockumentary that came out that same year. The films overlapped in depicting Jews as the scum of the earth, *Untermenschen* bent on laying waste to the world, with their "crown," in Hitler's words, "becoming the funeral wreath of humanity." Absent the pomp and circumstance of *Jud Süss* and zero entertainment value, *The Eternal Jew* was a horrifying, pitiless assault on the Jews, so much so that their creators refrained from showing it in regular theaters. Scenes depicting Jews as rats crawling out of the sewer "in massing hordes" spreading disease might not go over well with the public and possibly backfire, "exciting the power of pity" (Quintilian) rather than its opposite – capital fare for SS Death Head Units and their ilk but unsuitable for the vulgus. As in *Jud Süss*, viewers were put on red alert not to be taken in by appearances, for no matter how much Jews resembled their Aryan counterparts, they were really "eternal Jews, bacilli in the host people." "Here's what real Jews look like," intoned the voiceover, depicting captured Polish Jews resembling hideous scarecrows. Jews were pimps, bloodsuckers, dope peddlers, child killers, sexual deviants, and purveyors of degenerate art. Ritual slaughter was nothing other than ritual torture, as Jews let live animals bleed to death and called it "humane slaughter." Sensitive viewers were bidden to look away.

Yet the fact that films like *Jud Süss* and *The Eternal Jew* were made at all shows that the regime understood that indiscriminate support for the persecution of the Jews, let alone their annihilation (which was

---

1. Cited in Jacob Boas, *We Are Witnesses: Five Diaries of Teenagers Who Died in the Holocaust* (New York: Square Fish/Macmillan, 2009), 93–94.

to be kept secret), was far from absolute and that not every German was on board with the Nazi resolution of the Jewish Question. If Jews and "Aryans" belonged to discrete species there would have been no need for films like *Jud Süss* and *The Eternal Jew*; no need for the Nuremberg Laws (1935) forbidding sex and marriage between Jews and non-Jews; no need to define the Jew; no need, after 1938, for Jewish men and women who didn't have an "approved" Jewish first name to take "Jewish-sounding" middle names like "Israel" and "Sara." Passports stamped with the letter "J" would have been unnecessary, as would elaborate cover stories to justify the most heinous of crimes against them.

On June 25, 1935, Minister of Propaganda Joseph Goebbels delivered a speech assailing those who dared intimate that Jews, too, were human beings. Six years later, Goebbels contributed an editorial to *Das Reich*, the flagship of the Nazi press, justifying the anti-Jewish measures: "how sad," he lamented, "compared with this international problem [the Jewish question] which has bothered mankind for millennia, are the stupid, sentimentally thoughtless arguments of some still extant pals of the Jews."[2] The pogrom of November 9/10, 1938, *Kristallnacht*, "the night of shattered glass," failed to excite most Germans, least of all the insurance companies saddled with the payout.

---

2. https://research.calvin.edu/german-propaganda-archive/goeb1.htm (accessed February 15, 2022).

2. Heinrich Himmler –
"Each One Has His Decent Jew"

The fear that the fate meted out to Jews would arouse pity rather than murderous hatred was taken seriously. In October 1943, SS Chief Heinrich Himmler materialized in Poznan to gird up the loins of officers tasked with overseeing the routines of destruction in Poland. For cruelty seemed to have sprung a leak. Pity rushed in, taking the architects of the Final Solution by surprise. "... I want to also mention a very difficult subject, ... with complete candor," Himmler stated, homing in on the nub of his discourse. "It should be discussed amongst us, yet nevertheless, we will never speak about it in public...

> I am talking about the evacuation of the Jews, the extermination of the Jewish people. It is one of those things that is easily said. 'The Jewish people is being exterminated,' every Party member will tell

you 'perfectly clear, it's part of our plans, we're eliminating the Jews, exterminating them, a small matter.' And then along they all come, all the 80 million upright Germans, and each one has his decent Jew. They say: all the others are swine, but here is a first-class Jew… none of them has seen it, has endured it.

Most of you will know what it means when 100 bodies lie together, when 500 are there or when there are 1,000. And… to have seen this through and – apart from human weakness – to have remained decent, has made us hard and is a page of glory never mentioned and never to be mentioned. Because we know how difficult things would be, if today in every city during the bomb attacks, the burdens of war and privations, we still had Jews as secret saboteurs, agitators, and troublemakers. We would probably be at the same stage as 16/17 [1916/17], if the Jews still resided in the body of the German people.[3]

3. Amsterdam, February 9, 1941

In the afternoon of Sunday, February 9, a gang of Dutch Nazis and off-duty German police foregathered at the Tilly bar on Rembrandt Square, a favorite hangout. Nothing easier than conjuring up the scene. Tanked up on Dutch Courage (gin), swaying on their bar stools, *Sieg-heiling*, hooting and hollering, they clinked glasses to the latest anti-Jewish decrees: Jews not allowed to go to the movies – CLINK!; Jewish doctors to register their religious affiliation and restricted to treating fellow Jews – CLINK! *Numerus clausus* in education – CLINK! CLINK! CLINK! CLINK!

In the early evening, done socializing, wielding hatchets and truncheons, the party faithful set out for the heart of the Jewish neighborhood, Waterloo Square, a short walk. "At 6:15," reported the neighborhood police,

> several unidentified civilians informed Officer Bookelman that shots were fired at the so-called flea market [Waterloo Square],

---

3. German and English at https://phdn.org/archives/holocaust-history.org /himmler-poznan/speech-text.shtml (accessed June 10, 2022).

reportedly by N.S.B.-men and German soldiers. Officer Ottema, accompanied by six other men from this station, headed out immediately, reinforced by 10 other officers dispatched from headquarters upon request. Upon their return, the officers confirmed the presence of N.S.B.-men, some in uniform, as well as several uniformed WA-men,[4] German soldiers, and off-duty *Grüne Polizei* [German Order Police]. The N.S.B.-men, armed with clubs smashed the windows of adjacent properties, assisted by off-duty German soldiers. Shots were fired by hitherto unidentified N.S.B.-men, as well as by the Germans…No one, as far as we know, was wounded.

TUESDAY, FEBRUARY 11

Expecting more of the same, neighborhood Jews organized Fighting Squads. Waterloo Square was transformed into a battleground in which Jews, joined by non-Jewish sympathizers, drove the Nazis from the square. A Dutch Nazi subsequently died of a headwound and was buried on the 17th. On the 19th, the N.S.B. showed up at a Jewish-owned ice cream parlor in South Amsterdam and was put to flight by gas released from an ammonia flask. Accused of running a Jewish terrorist group that used poison gas, part-owner Ernst Cahn was executed on March 3, becoming the first person in occupied Holland to die by firing squad.

FEBRUARY 22 AND 23. RAIDS IN THE JEWISH QUARTER[5]

Responding to the riots, armed *Grüne Polizei* went door to door yanking 389 Jewish men between the ages of 20 and 45 from their homes, arms raised. The men were taken to a nearby square under

---

4. N.S.B. – Nationaal Socialistische Beweging: Dutch National Socialist Movement. WA – Weerafdeling: military arm of the N.S.B.
5. The 389 men were the subject of an exhibition at Amsterdam's City Archive in the spring of 2022. https://www.amsterdam.nl/stadsarchief/themasites /razzia (accessed February 15, 2023). Based on Wally de Lang's *De razzia's van 22 en 23 februari 1941 in Amsterdam: het lot van 389 Joodse mannen* (The razzias of February 22 and 23 1941 in Amsterdam: the fate of 389 Jewish men) (Amsterdam/Antwerpen: Atlas Contact, 2021).

armed escort, abused, loaded onto trucks, and dispatched to a transit camp on the Dutch coast, thence to Buchenwald and Mauthausen. None survived.

FEBRUARY 25, 26.

Days later, Amsterdam workers went on strike in solidarity with the Jews. Quickly put down, the Germans instituted a Jewish Council responsible for maintaining order, on pain of further raids.

According to documents at the headquarters of the International Tracing Service of the Red Cross at Bad Arolsen, Germany, the occupier regarded the 389 men as political prisoners first and Jews second. They were treated like beasts of burden, without the benefits thereof. The practice amounted to being "worked to death" – *Vernichtung durch Arbeit*. Strapped to the "Jew Cart," with an overseer dictating the tempo – *Rück-Zwei-Drei-Vier. Rück-Zwei-Drei-Vier – Pull! Two-Three-Four. Pull-two-three-four* – they lugged tree trunks, stones, sand, pebbles, cement, and similar back-breaking toil. The food was abominable, and before long the men resembled skeletons. Letters sent home – one per month per prisoner and in German – were required to include the phrase *Es geht mir sehr gut – I am doing well,* or its variant *Alles steht uns zur Verfügung – All our needs are being met.* By May 22, 1941, 47 victims of the February raids had perished in Buchenwald. At the end of May, 340 survivors were transferred to Mauthausen, the stone-quarrying camp in Austria. Mauthausen was designated as "a third category" camp, signifying that no one would be allowed to remain alive."[6] Some prisoners, linking hands, jumped to their death in the quarry; others threw themselves against the electrified barbed wire. Death certificates recorded that an inmate had been "shot in the act of escaping." Incapacitated prisoners were killed in the gas chamber at nearby Hartheim Castle. This was done in the greatest secrecy.[7]

4. Joseph Dagloonder[8]

I don't know if Joseph Dagloonder was part of a neighborhood Fighting Squad. What I do know is that on the weekend of February 22/23 Dagloonder was one of the 389 men rounded up and dispatched to Buchenwald. He arrived on February 26 and died there two months thereafter. His Buchenwald camp card recorded that prisoner 3272 was a Dutch Jew, born December 10, 1908, in Amsterdam, barber by trade, married to Eva D. (Eva van West), and arrested by Amsterdam's SIPO (Himmler's Security Police). The card lists his belongings at the time of incarceration: hat, shoes, coat, socks, vest, two shirts, collar, studs, wallet, and plain ring. Not listed on the card are their two children Abraham and Jansje. Another card reported that he died of "consumption" (tuberculosis).

The address on the card erroneously listed Nieuwe Uilenburger-straat 119 rather than 119A-1. This is the same flat we moved into in February 1946, six months after our release from Transit Camp West-erbork. I was two years old. The building no longer exists. It was torn down in the early 1990s to make way for a modern apartment build-

---

6. De Lang, *De razzia's,* 207.

7. Ibid., 185; 187–193.

8. More on Joseph Dagloonder and family (in English), including photographs, at https://www.joodsmonument.nl/en/page/647062/joseph-dagloonder.

ing. In truth, it should have been demolished long before that. But I may be wrong, for I don't recall it being all that bad. Then again, I have no memory as to the shape it was in when we moved in, though years later and well past the "whining schoolboy" age my mother insisted that it was indeed condemned and that we were simply squatters. Be that as it may, it was a huge comedown from the flat my parents had moved into shortly after they married, November 1, 1939. The latter was in a neighborhood in East Amsterdam whose streets and squares paid homage to the vanquished Boers of South Africa. Their street was named after Danie Theron, "best known," according to Wikipedia, "as the driving force behind the formation of a military bicycle corps used by the Boer Army for scouting and relaying messages." In the Boer War, the Germans, like the Dutch, were on the side of the Afrikaners and may well have supplied the bicycles but left it to the British to pioneer the concentration camp. Did the Germans commandeer my parents' bicycles in 1942 to recoup the deficit? Only if you happen to believe that every epoch is equidistant from God, history is meaningless, or negate the existence of time altogether. Be that as it may, my parents' bicycles wound up in Germany, as would their household effects, touted as a gift from the empathetic Dutch to the victims of Allied bombing raids. No one there swallowed the cover story; everyone knew. Local leaders and party members had first pick, then the rank and file.[9]

Joseph Dagloonder was a typical product of the vanished Jewish neighborhood. One of six children, he was born there, attended school there, worked there, married there, helped raise two children there, and, presumably, would have grown old and died there. The third of six children (an older brother had died young), Joseph completed five years of elementary school, worked a clutch of odd jobs, and for some years toiled as a barber, the occupation registered on the Family Card (see below) and at Buchenwald. Joseph's military register established that he was 1 m 72.5 cm tall and best suited to serve his

9. See Peter Junk and Martina Sellmeyer. *Stationen auf dem Weg nach Auschwitz: Entrechtung, Vertreibung, Vernichtung, Juden in Osnabrück 1900 – 1945. Ein Gedenkbuch* (Osnabrück: Rach Verlag Bramsche, 1988) (Stations on the road to Auschwitz: disenfranchisement, expulsion, annihilation), 258.

country in a cycling capacity. In 1934, Joseph teamed up with his father, Abraham Dagloonder, hawking fruit in the center of Amsterdam's Jewish quarter; the following year, they sold flowers and plants in West Amsterdam. There are four photographs attached to a vending license, ambulant and stationary. His market card for 1941 was stamped with a red J. In August 1941 Jews could no longer obtain new licenses, and the following month were banned from outdoor markets altogether. By then Joseph was no longer among the living.

Eleven percent of the 389 prisoners listed street vending as their economic mainstay.[10] Street vendors put in long hours. Up before the crack of dawn to collect their daily haul of perishables, fruit, flowers, and plants, pulling and pushing until the bulk had been sold, frequently until well into the evening. The law prohibited vendors from stopping, other than for making a sale, or risk getting fined; now and then the police would settle for a bribe in kind. A day in jail working off fines was a reasonable alternative. It was a hardscrabble existence, but it wasn't Buchenwald or Mauthausen.

In the spring of 2022, Joseph Dagloonder's ordeal and that of the 388 men seized in the February raids was the subject of an exhibit at the Amsterdam City Archives.[11] The exhibit consisted of short bios, photographs, dates of birth and death. The makers of the exhibit had at their disposal a variety of documents with which to reconstruct a semblance of the lives of the 389 men.

A critical source of information was the Family Card. Starting in 1893, every Amsterdam resident was registered on a Family Card. The card recorded the details of every family member: husband, wife, children, and any relatives living with the family, as well as their home address, and changes of address where applicable. According to the information on the card, Eva and the children moved to 66-III across the street from their previous address on April 7, 1941. Boxes 3 and

---

10. Occupations: 66 merchants/businessmen, self-employed; second highest total were peddlers/vendors: 43; 7 barbers; painters; wallpaper hanger; plumber, diamond worker, hatmaker, carpenter; 8 musicians, tap dancer, dancing instructor, photographer; doctor, religious teacher, teacher, druggist, real estate agent; student of medicine, clothing manufacturer. De Lang, *De razzia's*, 298–299.
11. See fn. 5.

4 furnished the particulars about Joseph, name, date, place of birth, and nationality. Box 6, blacked out after the war, gives the person's religious affiliation, in Dagloonder's case, "Isr."; (7) occupation, barber, the "o" specifies that Joseph was an employee rather than employer; (8) names of parents; (9) name of wife; (11) and (12) Eva's date and place of birth, April 2, 1908, Amsterdam; (13) date and place of marriage, December 9, 1931, Amsterdam. (21) and (22) furnish dates of changes of residence and current address. The flip side of the card registered the names of their children. Some of boxes have been blacked out, mostly for reasons of privacy. Nor is every entry necessarily accurate, least of all those entered during the war. In 1939, a Personal Card and Archive Card augmented the Family Card and other existing paperwork (Housing Card, Market Card, Alien Card, and Military Register). Place and date of death, top center, was added after the war; in Joseph's case, Buchenwald, April 26, 1941.

At the time of the German invasion, Holland's Population Registry was the most advanced tracking service in the world. The ramified bureaucratic panopticon in part accounts for the high percentage of murdered Jews, roughly 75 % of 140,000.[12]

---

12. Amsterdam's civil registry office was attacked by the resistance in March 1943, resulting in a partial destruction of its contents. The registry was also used to identify non-Jews earmarked for forced labor and other vile ends. Twelve

Despite the information at our fingertips, we don't get to know the real Joseph, or any of the other 388 men, through no fault of the makers of the exhibit at the Amsterdam City Archive.[13] What was he like? As a father, husband? What did he talk about at home? Did he have friends? Was he religious? Did he read a newspaper? If so, which? What were his political beliefs, provided he had any. In other words, what was he *really* like? We'll never know.

Eva was notified of her husband's death within days. On the first of May, she wrote a letter to Buchenwald's commandant requesting Joseph's belongings be sent back to her. These arrived at the SS headquarters in Amsterdam on May 13. The urn with his ashes followed suit. Joseph Dagloonder was buried in a Jewish cemetery on July 7. No one was allowed to be present at the ceremony, not even Eva.

The Dagloonder children, Abraham and Jansje, attended the J.D. Meyer elementary school across the street, the same school I attended between 1950 and 1956, when it was called De Oude Schans School. They and their mother were murdered in Sobibor in April 1943. Transport 57 – 2,020 prisoners, including 280 children, 34 cattle cars – pulled out of Westerbork on Tuesday, April 6, arriving on the 9th. A letter concealed in the train described the three-day journey.

> The first day of the journey was already horrible. The wagon was chockful. To use the bathroom, one had to climb over others. This is especially hard on the sick that need help getting out of bed. The mood is terrible. Everyone bickers and quarrels. When the door is shut, it stinks horribly, and the air gets stuffier and stuffier. With the door open, there's an enormous draft. It's pitch-dark. The night is unbearably cold, dreadful. When the doors are opened in the morning it feels like we're in the middle of winter. We encounter

of the attackers paid for the attack with their lives. Most of the attackers were subsequently caught and executed.
http://stadsarchief.amsterdam.nl/presentaties/amsterdamse_schatten/oproer/aanslag_bevolkingsregister/index.nl.html
13. https://www.amsterdam.nl/stadsarchief/themasites/razzia/joseph-dagloonder/ (accessed April 10, 2022).

prisoners of war, Russians, who wave a friendly hello.…We didn't sleep. The Greens [German police] are considerate and friendly. It's not so bad. At the various stations they supply us with water, bread, sausage, and ham. We passed Breslau.…We are totally beat. Still, Jewish humor is indomitable. Jokes are still being cracked, despite everything. By morning we are no longer moving. It seems that the tracks have been bombed and we are being rerouted, so the journey will take much longer. I can't face the prospect of a third night because we haven't changed our clothes, haven't washed, and haven't had anything warm to eat and drink. It's awful. In many places we now see prisoners of war toiling, such as splitting and hauling bricks, pushing carts, etc. under German supervision. The countryside is beautiful.…Strangely enough, we see few people and no cattle at all. Besides, Poland seems very poor.…We are 100 km from Lublin, so we'll arrive this evening. It has taken us three days and two nights. A horrific journey. The Polish farmer said that Jews were shot. We are hoping for a better fate.

Survivor Saartje Engel-Wijnberg.

…[W]e were selected upon arrival. Some men were selected for labor, as well as 28 young girls, including myself.…All the girls ate and slept communally. A revolt broke out led by Russian and Polish camp inmates against the German SS, triggered by a rumor that all of us would be shot on October 16, 1943. All prisoners, except thirty, were murdered. I only saw one of those girls again. My camp job was sorting out the rucksacks and clothes of the gassed. I know for certain that our entire transport, besides the 28 women and the men mentioned earlier, were immediately gassed upon arrival.

And:

After the men and women were separated thirty young women and seventy men were selected for work in Lager 2, where Ober-scharführer [Hermann] Michel said that after delousing they'd be sent to the Ukraine. The women had to undress in barracks and the men outdoors in a field. Unaware of what was about to happen, they and the children were taken to the gas chambers in Lager 3. That same evening, I had to dance for [Franz] Frenzel, accompanied by an accordion. I wasn't aware yet that Sobibor was a camp where people were being gassed.[14]

Abraham Dagloonder reached the age of 10 years.
Jansje Dagloonder reached the age of 8 years.
Eva Dagloonder van West was 35 years old.[15]

5. Operation Furniture's Final Solution

"We have taken away the riches that they had," Himmler concluded the speech he held in Poznan in October 1943,

> and ... I have given strict orders, which Obergruppenführer Pohl has carried out, we have delivered these riches to the Reich, to the State. We have taken nothing from them for ourselves. A few, who have offended against this, will be judged in accordance with an order that I gave at the beginning: he who takes even one Mark of this is a dead man. A number of SS men have offended against this order. They are very few, and they will be dead men WITHOUT MERCY! We have the moral right, we had the duty to our people, to kill this people who would kill us. We however do not have the right to enrich ourselves with even one fur, with one

---

14. Selections from Jules Schelvis, *Vernietigingskamp Sobibor* (Extermination Camp Sobibor), cited in Guus Luijters, *In Memoriam: De gedeporteerde en vermoorde Joodse, Roma en Sinti kinderen 1942–1945* (The deported and murdered Jewish, Roma and Sinti children, 1942–1945) (Amsterdam: Nieuw Amsterdam Uitgevers, 2012), 419–20.
15. Additional research established that the Dagloonders' downstairs and next-door neighbors had been murdered as well. Until they moved across the street, the downstairs flat at 119-A had been rented to Louis and Engeltje Cousin and their three children. Like Joseph Dagloonder, "political prisoner" Louis Cousin was arrested in February 1941 and three months later died in Buchenwald of "sepsis of the right thigh." The rest of the family, including J.D. Meyer school attendees Abraham and Maurice, were gassed at Sobibor May 28, 1943.

Mark, with one cigarette, with one watch, with anything. That we do not have. Because we don't want, at the end of all this, to get sick and die from the same bacillus that we have exterminated. I will never see it happen that even one … bit of putrefaction comes in contact with us, or takes root in us. On the contrary, where it might try to take root, we will burn it out together. But altogether we can say: We have carried out this most difficult task for the love of our people. And we have suffered no defect within us, in our soul, in our character.

ALFRED ROSENBERG

On 14 January 1942 – No. 001 364/R/Ma – the Reichsminister, Reichsleiter ROSENBERG, ordered the Staff of Reichsleiter ROSENBERG for the occupied territories "to safeguard furniture in Jewish households in the occupied WESTERN territories for the purpose of supplying the administration in the occupied territories of the East."[16]

The Dagloonder flat consisted of a kitchen with a toilet at the far end, a living room and bedroom separated by an alcove. No built-in closets, no hot water. The only source of heat was a stove in the living room. Documents pertaining to their household effects, the objects they touched, drank from, slept, sat, and breathed on went the way of the flat's occupants. *Erst kommt der Jude, dann die Möbel* – "First the Jew, then the furniture." At some point, a German task force styled Möbel-Aktion, or M-Aktion – "Operation Furniture" – entered the sealed off premises to assess the value of their household effects: clothing, dishware, pots, pans, tchotchkes; whatever. Under the circumstances, it would be safe to assume that smaller items of value wound up in the pockets of the assessors – if it weren't for Himmler's assurances that not a single *Pfennig* had gone to enrich those entrusted with the sacred task of ridding Europe of Jews. Signing off on the room-by-room inventory were a mover and a policeman, both Dutch, "very reliable and politically beyond reproach."

---

16. Declassified per Executive Order 12958, Section 3.5. NND Project Number: NND 775057. By: NND Date: 1977.

Möbel-Aktion was a Nazi looting enterprise attached to Einsatzstab Reichsleiter Rosenberg (ERR), Task Force Rosenberg, a "subtly interwoven spider web and an entangled mesh operating...across Europe, with its central hub in Berlin."[17] "Mesh" – and a fine one at that – is about right, as every item, from the most valuable art to the lowliest saltshaker was grist for the mill. With *Möbelfrei* the natural spawn of making Europe *Judenfrei*, the household effects of the Dagloonders, be it at 119A-1 or the flat Eva and her children moved into after Joseph's arrest, were to be stripped clean off everything but dirty underwear. Absent an itemized list, we do not know how they lived as we do for some of their neighbors. And while much has been made about Nazi-looted art and other cultural property, the items Operation Furniture reported to headquarters in Berlin have yet to be mentioned in the same breath as Gustav Klimt's *Portrait of Adele Bloch-Bauer I*.

By the time the moving van showed up to transfer the loot to the harbor for storage and shipment to Germany, a good deal of it might already have found a new home with neighbors beating the Germans to the punch or deposited for safekeeping. "Better us than they." Storing one's possessions with neighbors or acquaintances was strictly forbidden, as the Jewish Council impressed upon the about-to-be-deported; violators could end up in a concentration camp! Thieves, too, if caught, were held to account, but hardly to the same extent. My parents, for example, left some of their belongings with neighbors, including a rug. When they returned from the camps to reclaim their things, their former neighbors, claiming poverty, insisted on keeping them.

---

17. Eric Ketelaar, "Unravelling the Mesh: The ERR Survey as a Finding Aid." Paper presented at the Jewish Historical Museum, Amsterdam, October 19, 2011, 1. https://www.obs-traffic.museum/sites/default/files/ressources/files/Ketelaar_Unravelling_the_Mesh.pdf (accessed January 10, 2023).

6. "Het adres"[18]

In Marga Minco's short story "Het adres" (The address), a young woman who survived the war in hiding visits the couple that has been safeguarding a good deal of her murdered family's belongings, including fine China and silverware. "I wanted to see them, touch them, recognize them." The first time she showed up, the "keeper" wouldn't let her in, clearly troubled that she was back. The second time, the keeper's daughter invited her to wait for her mother, who was out shopping. The girl pours tea from their former teapot with the gold trim, served on the tablecloth with the small hole on the edge that was never mended. A small spoon emerges from a vintage antique box. When the girl is about to open the drawer with the silverware, the visitor gets up and leaves abruptly. To catch a train, she said.

> At the corner of the street, I took note of the street's name: it said Marconistraat. I had been at number 46. The address was correct. But now I no longer wanted to remember it. I wouldn't go back again, because the objects that are part of one's memory, of the familiar past, suddenly lose their value when you confront them again, torn from their context, in unfamiliar surroundings....I resolved to forget the address. Of all the things I needed to forget, this would have to be the easiest by far.[19]

---

18. Marga Minco: *Verzamelde verhalen: 1951–1981* (Collected stories: 1951–1981) (Amsterdam: Uitgeverij Bert Bakker, 1982), 46–51. Marga Minco, Dutch author best known for *Het bittere kruid* (*Bitter Herbs*). See also Chapter v, "Writers Guild."

19. Ibid., 51. The (non-itemized) yield in my deported paternal grandparents' apartment included a bicycle, laundry, shoes, clothes, and assorted furniture, totaling 80 guilders. Theirs was but one of the 30,000 looted Jewish households "safeguarded" in German-occupied Holland. "The dagger was literally replaced by the bureaucrat's pen, but this pen actually did a better job." Gerard Aalders, *Roof: De ontvreemding van joods bezit tijdens de Tweede Wereldoorlog* (Den Haag. SdU Uitgevers, 1999), 12. *Nazi looting. The Plunder of Dutch Jewry during the Second World War* (Oxford: New York, 2004).

7. Inventory Register

The top right-hand corner of the document registering the intake of the household effects of Raphaël Prins, Nieuwe Uilenburgerstraat 48-III, indicates that the building was the property of *Handwerkers Vriendenkring*, Craftsmen Circle of Friends, a non-profit tasked with improving the living conditions in this predominantly Jewish neighborhood in association with the municipal government. The top left-hand corner states that Raphaël Prins was Dutch and that the household consisted of two occupants. However, his wife's name, Mietje Prins-Pront, is not recorded on the document, and neither is that of their live-in son, Hartog Prins. Hartog had been rounded up that fatal February weekend and died in Mauthausen on September 18, 1941. Raphaël, barber by trade, was murdered in Auschwitz, September 30, 1942, aged 55, as was Mietje Prins-Pront, January 21, 1943, aged 51.[20]

THE HOME CONSISTS OF: 1 hallway, 4 rooms, 1 closet, 1 kitchen.

Room 1 contains the following furniture: linoleum floor covering, 1 carpet, 2 runners, 1 mirror, 5 vases, 1 table with tablecloth, 5 chairs, 2 armchairs, 1 sideboard with glass crockery, 1 radio, 1 shelf, 1 alarm clock, 1 couch with cover/blanket, 1 flower stand, 1 flower stand, 1 bird cage; cupboard, coffee and tea dishes.

TOTAL VALUE, HFL. 200.–[21]

ROOM 2: Linoleum floor covering, 1 mat, 2 curtains and 2 drapes, 1 hanging lamp, 1 wall plate, 1 wall painting, 1 oil painting, 1 stone figurine, 1 wooden bed with bedding, one round table with tablecloth, 3 chairs, 1 linen cabinet; closet with women's clothes, 2 oil stoves.

TOTAL VALUE: HFL. 150.–

ROOM 2: Storage room contains the following furniture: linoleum floor covering, 1 carpet, 1 mat, 2 curtains and two (sets of) drapes, 1 mirror, 1 hanging lamp, nick-nacks, 1 flower stand, 1 round table, 4 chairs, 1 easy chair, 1 armchair, 2 wall pictures.

TOTAL VALUE: HFL. 40.–

BEDROOM: Linoleum floor covering, 2 mats, 2 curtains and 2 drapes, 1 wall picture, 1 hanging lamp, 1 floor lamp, 1 wooden bedstead with bedding, one bookshelf with books, 2 chairs, contents, 1 closet with women's clothing.

TOTAL VALUE: HFL. 35.–

20. NIOD_093a_33_00018.jp. Einsatzstab Reichsleiter Rosenberg (NIOD: Instituut voor Oorlogs-, Holocaust- en Genocidestudies).
21. Hfl = Guilder. F Hfl. 200 = approximate value in today's euros 1,400.

HALLWAY: linoleum floor covering, 1 mat, 1 hanging lamp, 1 brush rack, 1 clothes stand, 1 umbrella stand; 2 chairs, 1 wall covering, closet with some clothing, 1 stepladder.

TOTAL VALUE: HFL. 10.–

Room 3 contains the following: KITCHEN: linoleum floor covering, 1 mat/runner, 1 rug, 1 curtain and drape, 1 hanging lamp, 1 clock, 2 gas stoves, 1 mirror, 1 medicine cabinet, 1 cabinet with tableware, some groceries, kitchen stuff, 1 table with tablecloth, 1 chair.

TOTAL VALUE: HFL. 35.–

Effected in Amsterdam, 22-7-42. By: [H.H.J.] Striethorst, [C.] Hoving.

The Prins' flat was unusually well appointed, given the neighborhood. Many of the street's residents were poor, the pickings slim. The document does convey a sense of the kind of furniture that was in vogue, however; the proverbial hanging lamp, for one, and the linoleum floor covering – *balatum* – for another. Many an Operation Furniture document terminated with a laconic *besitzen nur Kleider und Unterwäsche* – "Own nothing but clothes and underwear," as in the case of Prins' neighbors "Rachel and Harry Schelvis, Nieuw Uilenburgerstraat 44-1. What happened to their furniture? Deposited with neighbors? Theft?

8. Alfred Rosenberg

Whoever sets out on a great journey, must leave old house-hold goods behind. – Alfred Rosenberg, *The Myth of the Twentieth Century.*

Overseeing the punctilio of the "Final Solution" for Jewish homes, works of art, and other cultural property in the Netherlands and throughout German-occupied Europe was Nazi ideologue Alfred Rosenberg. Rosenberg was born in 1893 and died 53 years later on the gallows at Nuremberg, 1:49 A.M., October 16, 1946, having been found guilty of "conspiracy to commit crimes against peace; planning, initiating and waging wars of aggression, war crimes, and crimes against humanity."

Rosenberg was the author of *The Myth of the Twentieth Century: An Evaluation of the Spiritual-Intellectual Confrontations of Our Age* (1930). Rosenberg's "myth" was the myth of white supremacy, the be-all and end-all of history. "In studying the history and literature of the Jews," Rosenberg declared, one finds almost nothing but energetic, endlessly busy activity, a completely one-sided concentration of all energies upon material well-being. From this veritable amoral disposition of spirit, a moral code originates which recognizes only one thing: The personal advantage of the Jew.... So, for 2,500 years we see eternally the same picture. Greedy for the goods of this world, the Jew moves from city to city, from land to land, and remains where he finds the least resistance to his parasitical business activity.... jugularly-like and half demonic, laughable and tragic at the same time, despising everything superior while nevertheless feeling himself innocent, we see that he is devoid of the capacity of being able to understand anything other than himself. Eternally he operates under the Satanic name ... forever a barren and condemned parasite.

America's racial insanity:

Fourteen million Negroes and mulattos, four to five million Jews, the Japanese in the west, and the rest, are more than America can carry without endangering the heritage of her pioneers. But if the present generation fails to do something to elude the fate of someday having twenty-five million Negroes and mulattos, and ten and a half million Jews in America, then a later generation will certainly be harsh in its judgment. The Americans will have to decide whether they want a white America or not.... Today every single American curses this Black liberation [in the southern states].... The Black question stands at the head of all questions of existence in the United States of America.... The yellow peril in California has likewise made the race problem a burning issue.... If the insane principle of the equality and equal rights of all races and religions is finally given up, there is yet hope.[22]

"Who was this rather quiet and withdrawn – even shy – man with the somewhat bland good looks of an upper-class English senior civil

---

22. Text on webpage of The Censure of the Democracy (no longer accessible), a neo-Nazi outfit. See also, https://en.metapedia.org/wiki/James _B._Whisker.

servant?" mused Holocaust denier Dr. Peter Peel of Reseda, California, in 1981.[23] "By all accounts he was, in his personal life, a kind man, rather humorless, incorruptible." "Rosenberg's view," explained Dr. Peel summarizing the ideologue's Weltanschauung, "is that the various races of man possess racial souls. These racial souls

> are as enduring and immutable as the racial phenotype – no more, no less. They give rise to cultures, values, religions and political systems which are uniquely congruent with the race in question, and are alien to any other race. Miscegenation brings about the degeneration and destruction of such cultures by reason of a kind of schizophrenic condition of racial bastardy. Aryan man has created all the great civilizations of ancient India, ancient Persia, Greece, Rome and, probably, Egypt. Each has ultimately decayed and failed by reason of racial mixing.… The Jew is the eternal enemy of Aryan values and Aryan culture.

"In 1940," Dr. Peel continues, Rosenberg "headed a special staff which had the responsibility

> of collecting and safeguarding the art treasures of the occupied eastern territories. This gave rise to the charge against him at Nuremberg of the wholesale looting of art treasures. It might be salutary to recall in passing that some 6,000 German painting were liberated by the American occupation authorities after World War II and shipped to the United States.… In 1941, Rosenberg was given the responsibility of setting up the civil administration of the occupied Russian and Baltic territories [Rosenberg was a Baltic German]. The appointment seems to have been – or soon to have become – a merely ceremonial position.

While waiting for the verdict at the Nuremberg War Crimes Tribunal and with no more furniture and art works to "safeguard," Rosenberg was at leisure to ponder his past and write his memoirs.

Composed in the shadow of the gallows, Rosenberg's *apologia pro*

---

23. "The Life and Death of Alfred Rosenberg." http://www.renegadetribune.com/the-life-and-death-of-alfred-rosenberg/ (accessed January 28, 2023).

vita sua reiterated the "philosophy" of the *Myth*, embellished with personal touches, like the fringe on a cheap carpet. He "looked upon life," he said, "from the vantage point of art – the art of the eye" – and in art, as in all things, moderation was "the basic law." "But essentially art was and is, in all its finer manifestations, a personal confession of faith, and never something tactical or political." As a young man he took part in a furniture design competition and placed first, he recalled. No Malthusian he: "The Volkswagen, was criticized by biologists and statisticians who claimed that each Volkswagen meant one child less. This seemed plausible enough."

Rosenberg was not without his enemies at the top. "In the Ministry of the East I was continually aware of Himmler's and Heydrich's political opposition." As for Goebbels: "During the Party Day of 1937, I, as the first among the living, received the new National Prize for Arts and Sciences. Inwardly seething but outwardly completely master of himself, Goebbels had to make the announcement that brought about a prolonged stamping of feet in approval."

Rosenberg last spoke to Hitler in 1942: "he esteemed me highly, but he did not love me." As for painting, "Hitler had strictly lower middle-class taste that frequently did not go beyond genre." The Führer's "great love" was architecture.

Unsurprisingly, in the memoir as in *The Myth*, the "eternal Jew" easily retained the inside track. The Jews' continued existence was an unmitigated disaster, the death knell of humanity. Unrepentant to the end, Rosenberg's political testament enshrined National Socialism as "the noblest of ideas" that would rise again.

"When Rosenberg's life and career are examined with impartiality and detachment," Dr. Peel concluded,

> one is forced to the conclusion that his real crime was racism and, more specifically, antisemitism. He was hanged, it would appear, for what he thought and wrote. The American prosecutor hammered away on this point. Rosenberg's writings, he charged, were instrumental in the rise of the Nazi party to power. It seems a strange sort of indictment coming from the representative of a power which is always so smugly self-congratulatory about the First Amendment.

9. Beyond Furniture

Although a major aspect of Rosenberg's Task Force in Holland was the seizure of Jewish household effects – *Haushalterfassung* – its tentacles spread well beyond scooping up flower and umbrella stands. In January 1940, for example, Rosenberg was tasked with establishing the Hohe Schule der NSDAP, the party's elite teaching and research institute. In 1942, hundreds upon hundreds of crates of books were dispatched to Berlin earmarked for the Hohe Schule. Seized cultural property was divided into four columns: name and address of the looted entity, number of crates, labeling, and content. Contents included holdings of Amsterdam's Anthropological, Theosophist, Neo-Malthusians, Spiritualist, Jehovah's Witnesses, Esperanto and Catholic societies as well as university and privately-owned Jewish libraries. Subjects included pacifism, occultism, psychical research, music and Marxist literature, art books, history, Spinoza's works, etc. etc. The Task Force's agents swept across the country, seizing shiploads of materials designed to upholster the regime's ideological infrastructure.

A particularly rich vein destined for the Hohe Schule was that of The Hague antiquarian H. Gotschalk. The first of 110 crates contained valuable historical works of Italian art and literature, specifically Leonardo da Vinci's *Traité de la Peinture*, 1671; a signed manuscript of Florian's opera "La Soubrette"; "Vocabulario Toscane dell Arte die dissegno," 1681; "Viaggio Pitteresco D'Italia", 1671; "Orus Apollo Milianus," 1538, Venice, as well as a first edition of Voltaire's *Antimachiavelli* (1740). The paperwork for crate 60 listed Cassel's *History of the United States* (3 volumes); Cassel's *History of England* (9 volumes); Macauley's *History of England* (2 volumes); Chamber's *Encyclopedia of English Literature* (2 volumes); Cotta's 1858 edition of Goethe's works (20 volumes); Breasted's *Geschichte Ägyptens*; Shakespeare in German (6 vols.); Motley's *Rise of the Dutch Republic,* and various original English works on English literature and history.[24]

---

24. NIOD (Institute for War, Holocaust and Genocide Studies), Archief 93a, Einsatzstab Rosenberg inv. No. 63. https://www.archieven.nl/nl/zoeken?mia

On January 18, 1941, Rosenberg was informed that the expropriation of the library of Amsterdam's Institute of Social Research, then
in its sixth year of existence, had been contractually secured. Two-
and-a-half years later, August 23, 1943, the Reichsleiter congratulated
the chief of the Main Working Group Netherlands, Party Comrade
Schmidt-Stähler, for having provisionally completed the organization
of the former institute's library.[25]

Task Force's monthly reports indicate that hundreds of thousands
of books from libraries, Jewish private book and art collections, synagogue holdings, antiquarians, as well as non-Jewish sites dedicated to
music, law, medicine, engineering, and so forth, wound up in Germany.
So much was stolen that the ERR headquarters in Amsterdam struggled to keep up with the flow. Requests routinely went out for more
shelf and storage space. The March 1943 report gives an indication of
the operation's scope in the Netherlands. The month's take included
the "so-called Napoleon Collection" of the German-Jewish emigrant
Loew who had committed suicide upon the German invasion. The
collection consisted of pictures and books centering on Napoleon
and his inner circle, brooches, and a silver cannister. The collection
was headed for Berlin.

The same document reported the acquisition of the Jewish Museum in Amsterdam. The museum, however, was no longer located in
Amsterdam but shipped to an underground air defense space in the
dunes near Zandvoort. According to the report, negotiations were un-
derway to take charge of the collection in April, pending resolution of
shipping difficulties. Additional items included the library of the Jew
Dr. Brasch, Amsterdam, Rijnstraat 1b. These contained some valuable
works, the report stated, but also much banned German writing pre-
dating 1933 that were of no interest to the Task Force.

Although work on Dutch libraries was being expanded, much
work remained unscrambling desirable from undesirable literature.
Unfortunately, neither the Literature Department of the Propaganda

---

dt=298&mizig=210&miview=inv2&milang=nl&micols=1&micode=093a
&mizk_alle=093a&mip2=63.

25. Ibid., Archief 93a, Einsatzstab Rosenberg, inv. No. 57.

Ministry, nor the state department for culture, nor the N.S.B., the document complained, had been as forthcoming as they should in supporting this important work. Nevertheless, the report concluded, the Task Force's card index of undesirable works had grown to 480 titles. The document then proceeded to describe the contents of seven crates, labeled by number, destined for the *Heimat*.[26]

10. Restitution

Restitution for stolen Jewish property is a complicated business, in the Netherlands as elsewhere, as hefty tomes on this subject go to prove.[27] To keep things simple, I'll stick close to home, i.e, the outcome of my parents' application requesting reimbursement for stolen household effects at their prewar address, Danie Theronstraat 34-ground floor. My parents applied in March of 1958. Section 1-a of the application form established that the loss of furniture was caused by "persecution on account of race, religion or political belief." The postwar reimbursement settlement fixed the total value of their stolen household goods on the day before the German invasion, May 9, 1940, at 1,479 (1957 guilders). Based on the formula worked out between the German Federal government, the Dutch Minister of Finance, and a consortium of Jewish agencies, they ultimately received 1,638.12 guilders, or 977 CAD – by then we were living in Canada. In 1960, one Canadian dollar was the equivalent of $8.86 CAD in 2021.

* * *

---

26. See NIOD, 51, 93a (Einsatzstab Reichsleiter Rosenberg), NIOD, Verslagen van activiteiten, 1943–1944) (Monthly reports of activities).
27. See Aalders, *Roof: De ontvreemding van joods bezit tijdens de Tweede Wereldoorlog* (Theft: The expropriation of Jewish assets in the Second World War) (Den Haag: SdU Uitgevers, 1999), 229–236 Joop Sanders, *Bittergeld: De restitutie van geroofde Joodse oorlogstegoeden* (Nederland: Verbum en Joop Sanders, 2022) (Bitter money: the restitution of looted Jewish assets).

Chapter 11
Death of an Era

Rootedness is perhaps the least understood need of the human soul.   – Simone Weil

1. Pegasus

In 2011, Dutch scholars compiled a list of 211 ex libris of German-Jewish exiles in the Netherlands, 1933–1940, opening what they called "a small window into history other sources might have overlooked or barely cover." "We are aware," they add, "that for many of these it's about the past in the shadow of persecution and war, which is why the 'In Memoriam' quotient is rather high."[1]

An ex libris, the authors write elsewhere, is "an artfully designed ownership brand pasted inside a book either to embellish, to protect against theft, impart a personal character trait, or as something to pass on to the next generation in memory of the original titulary."[2] Many

---

1. Jan Aarts, F.J. Hoogewoud, and Chris Kooyman, *Ex libris in exil: duits-joodse vluchtelingen in Nederland 1933–1940* (Ex libris in exile: German-Jewish refugees in the Netherlands) (Amsterdam: De Buitenkant, volume 14, No. 2/3/2011), 26–27.
2. Jan Aarts & Chris Kooyman (with a contribution by F.J. Hoogewoud), *Dit is mijn boek: Joodse exlibriscultuur* in Nederland (Amsterdam: De Buitenkant, 2017) (This is my book: Jewish ex libris culture in the Netherlands), 15. This volume incorporates the ex libris of German-Jewish exiles in the above-mentioned publication.

of the ex libris, they note, were found among the books "appropriated" by Task Force Rosenberg.

Georg Hermann Borchardt had not one but two ex libris. The first has a pile of books rising like a skyscraper in the center of a city amid higgledy-piggledy dwellings. Atop this pile a man sits astride a rearing Pegasus, the winged horse of poetry. The equestrian is Georg Hermann Borchardt. The authors contend that the ex libris represents Borchardt as a successful author, best known for the novels *Jettchen Gebert* (1906) and its sequel, *Henriëtte Jacoby* (1908), both published under his nom de plume, Georg Hermann. The jumbled dwellings, they add, are characteristic of the expressionistic style of Erich Büttner (1889–1936), painter, graphic artist, commercial artist, illustrator, and denote Berlin, the setting of many a Hermann book. "Büttner designed more than 200 ex libris, approaching the titularies from a psychological angle as though to reveal something about their souls as well as their city."[3]

---

3. Ibid., 135.

Borchardt's second ex libris consists of a dark-green flat space inside a pentagon inscribed with the letters "ex libris" and the name of the titulary. Top and bottom depict decorative chains of beads and glass crystals in Jugendstil (by an unknown designer). This ex libris references Hermann's collection of antiques and curiosities. Having fled to the Netherlands after Hitler's seizure of power, the writer filled his house in Hilversum with art objects – open to visitors in the morning. This gave Borchardt a tax break. The ex libris came from Frau Marie Grubbe by Danish author J.P. Jacobson, a Borchardt favorite.

Additional details bear on Borchardt's personal life: married Martha Heynemann (1875–1954). Daughters: Eva Maria (1903); Hilde (Mulle) (1904); and Elise (Liese) (1906). Divorced in 1918. Married Lotte Samter (died 1926). Daughter: Ursula Henriëtte (Uschschen) (1919).

Hermann's "sanitized" autobiography in 193 words:

I was born in 1871 as the youngest son of Jewish parents. My mother came from a distinguished Berlin family. I grew up in West Berlin and attended various schools. I was interested, at a very young age, in natural sciences, collecting plants, beetles, and butterflies. Most likely inspired by Turgenev, as well by Dickens and Andersen, my first literary ventures involved competing with a fellow student with a literary bent. I became a business type but remained true to my literary calling, finding time during my military service to complete my first novel. Attended Berlin University between my twenty-fifth and twenty-eighth year, primarily focusing on art history; became a newspaper art critic, and after five years of keeping a low profile wrote a novel [*Jettchen Gebert*] – the fifth – that made my name. I married, was blessed with three children, lived a simple, quiet life, and was successful. There you have the official, sanitized, conventional biography. Somewhat less officially, it wasn't quite so conventional and respectable as all that.[4]

---

4. *Het Salamanderboek* (Amsterdam: N.V. EM Querido Uitgeversmaatschappij, 1938), 83–87. Also cited in https://www.joodsmonument.nl/nl/page/381828/georg-hermann-borchardt-autobiografisch.

2. Exile

Between 1933 and the invasion of the Netherlands in May 1940, thousands of German Jews streamed into the Netherlands, overwhelmingly concentrated in Amsterdam. Many stayed no more than a day or two before moving on to other countries. A head count in 1941 put the number of German Jews in Holland at 20,000.

The influx of German authors turned Amsterdam into a mecca of German exile publishing, thanks largely to two Amsterdam publishers, Em. Querido and Allert de Lange.[5] The former created a separate German-language publishing unit, the latter a "division." Until 1940, they published some 200 émigré German-language authors, many, like Hermann, with a track record in the Netherlands: Irmgard Keun, Joseph Roth, Alfred Döblin, Vicki Baum, Heinrich Mann, Lion Feuchtwanger, Anna Seghers, Bertolt Brecht, and Klaus Mann, among others. Other border-crossing footprints led to a German coffee-shop, deli, tearoom, bookstore, bakery, theaters, and concert halls.

Overall, German Jews were not liked by the Dutch – German, all too German. And some Dutch Jews disliked them as well. There was a feeling that the better educated and more prosperous German Jews with their profound love of things German looked down their noses at their Dutch co-religionists.

Georg Hermann Borchardt (henceforth Georg Hermann) entered Holland following the Reichstag Fire of February 27, 1933. Holland was a good fit. Dutch translations of his books were widely read, and between 1921 and 1926 he wrote a weekly column reviewing German literature for a Dutch newspaper.[6] There were few obstacles barring entry; no need to apply for a visa, as in France, say. Culturally, the two countries were close. German had been taught in Dutch schools since the middle of the nineteenth century. There was the reputation for

---

5. See Bettina Baltschev, *Hel en Paradijs: Amsterdam en de Duitse exilliteratuur,* trans. Mark Wildschut (Amsterdam: Antwerpen, Querido, 2017).

6. See Laureen Nussbaum, "A Sampling of Georg Hermann's 'Letters about German Literature,' *Algemeen Handelsblad 1921–1926,*" in *Georg Hermann: Deutsch-jüdischer Schriftsteller und Journalist, 1871–1943* (Halle and Tübingen: Max Niemeyer Verlag, 2004), 73–86.

tolerance. The country hadn't experienced war, revolution, inflation. It was a bit like entering a country where it was still 1912, recalled fellow German-Jewish refugee Werner Cahn.[7]

GEORG HERMANN "CHATS"

In 1937, Hermann was interviewed by Dutch cultural critic Menno ter Braak. The interview took place in the lobby of the Princesse Schouwburg (Theater) in The Hague, where an operetta based on the novel *Jettchen Gebert* was hours away from having its premiere.[8] Somehow, Ter Braak remarked, the novel had become compounded with the "racial question."

> It is an old gentleman, the writer Georg Hermann, whom I had never met in person.... Perhaps better qualified as "little old gentle-man," because he really is quite short, and most affable indeed. You probably already know that Herman is a collector of art. Well, his entire demeanor, his conversation and his way of thinking is that of a collector, whose approach to literature is equally discerning, flitting from one topic to another – a choosy type but quite an expert, nonetheless. His humor and sheer chattiness betrayed 'a real Berliner'; a man of table-talks for the sake of table-talks who not only relishes his own anecdotes, but also their delivery, which is the hallmark of a true collector, an eye for detail.... The pleasure in talking, the art of moving from subject to subject without ever being at a loss for a punchline; the amusing extempore conversa-tion, the quaint bonhomie – that's Georg Hermann. These days we rarely encounter such cultivated nonchalance, and Hermann confesses outright that the literature of younger authors who are into hard-boiled realism doesn't impress him. In the contemporary novel, he says, there is a surfeit of action. The tranquility, the

---

7. Cited in Philo Bregstein and Salvador Bloemgarten, *Herinnering aan Joods Amsterdam* (Remembering Jewish Amsterdam) (Amsterdam: Uitgeverij De Bezige Bij, 1978), 261. Cahn came to Holland in 1934 and joined the staff of Amsterdam publisher EM. Querido.
8. "Georg Hermann 'Plaudert,'" *Het Vaderland*, March 16, 1937.

attention to the milieu is missing, as is the mood relished by the avid reader. This is the standpoint, once more, of a collector, who wants to enjoy his beloved possessions with a serene, epicurean fondness.… One senses that Georg Hermann could go on forever in this stream of anecdotes and aperçus,… a Berlin horn of plenty. This evening Hermann will attend the operetta's premiere. The operetta, he says getting up to leave, must follow the book's conversation as accurately as possible. 'In truth, all you need to turn a novel into an operetta is a good pair scissors.'

3. Jettchen Gebert

Historians flag the years between the end of the Napoleonic Wars in 1815 and the Revolution of 1848 as the *Biedermeier* era. This was a time of peace, growing industrialization, urbanization, rising middle class, and new directions in the arts. Hermann made Biedermeier Berlin the nostalgic focus of his antique collection and the setting of his novel *Jettchen Gebert* (1906). The novel was a big hit, as was its sequel *Henrietta Jacoby* (1908), both were made into films, and both premiered in Berlin in 1918.

Jetchen Gebert – twenty-five, bookish, blonde, beautiful – lives with her aunt and uncle, Salomon and Rikchen Gebert. Uncle Salomon runs a profitable textile and silk fabrics business, Salomon Gebert & Co. The setting is Berlin, 1839. The Geberts are Jews, beneficiaries of Prussia's 1812 Edict of Emancipation. The fact that between 1812 and 1845 thousands of Jews took out baptismal certificates – their *Entréebillet* to European culture (Heinrich Heine) – indicates that the edict didn't quite go far enough. The Geberts, too, could have converted, added a *von* to their name, become army officers and councilors of state, but opted to remain Jews. "That is our pride, and we really wouldn't want that to change, would we? You understand that, right"? Uncle Jason forewarns wannabe suitor Herr Doktor Fritz Kössling. The fact that the Geberts are incorrigibly bourgeois cut off yet another pass. PhD in literature, non-Jewish, low income, scraping by writing for magazines, Herr Doktor simply lacked the *Entréebillet* to their world. Even so, Jason promised to plead his friend's case. To no avail.

Jettchen and Fritz first met at an extended family dinner at the Geberts' that Jason had invited Herr Doktor to share. Unsurprisingly, the latter felt out of place; theirs was one world, his another, and that was that.

> The people here had come to terms with life as they found it. They were so distressingly satiated. What, after all, did they lack? They had enough and didn't ask for more. Eating, drinking, music, literature, the house filled every need. The frustration, the existential angst that roiled him, the bitter with the sweet, were completely alien to them. What was he doing here?

Jettchen, though, is already spoken for, provided a Jewish suitor materializes to fill the bill. "By *uns* kommt *keiner* los van der Familie, bei *uns* nicht" (emphasis in the original) – "No one, but no one can break with the family, not ever, not with us," Jettchen tells Kössling. On a long, unchaperoned walk, they confess their love, embrace, kiss.

"Und alles kam, wie es kommen musste, alles, wie es kommen musste" – "And everything came to pass as it had to, everything." An acceptable suitor does indeed materialize; acceptable, that is, to the Geberts: Julius, a consummate bore and not nearly the successful businessman he makes himself out to be. The pressure exerted on Jettchen, who can't abide Julius, is relentless; and she caves. The alternatives – remain single or opt for Christianity and marry Kössling – are non-starters. The book's finale documents Jettchen's unfathomable unhappiness, offset momentarily by a brief, passionate encounter with Kössling. Clearly, Jettchen is fated to spend the rest of her days entombed in a sumptuous Berlin home, trapped in a loveless marriage and endless rounds of family fixtures.

4. "Fabrizius"

Hermann's interviewer Menno ter Braak paid a great deal of attention to émigré literature, much of it by Jews, opening his newspaper's cultural pages to their offerings. He was not impressed, accusing refugee novelists of rehashing the old while the times went begging for something rather more relevant, and defaulting rather too often to historical novels, a genre he despised. For the most part, however, the cultural critic left the task of reviewing émigré literature to Mallorca-based German author and translator Albert Vigoleis Thelen (1903–1989). The result was *Duitsche Letteren in den Vreemde* – German literature abroad. Over the next six years, signing off as Leopold Fabrizius, Thelen reviewed 143 books, including four by Hermann: *Ruths schwere Stunde* (1934); *Rosenemil* (1935); *Der unbekannte Fussgänger* (1935), and *Der etruskische Spiegel* (1936).[9]

---

9. Between 1931 and the outbreak of the Spanish Civil War in 1936, Albert Vigoleis Thelen resided in Mallorca, the setting for *Die Insel des Zweiten Gesichts: aus den angewandten Errinerungen Vigoleis* (Amsterdam: Van Oorschot, 1953). *The Island of Second Sight. From the Applied Recollections of Vigoleis*, trans. Donald O. White (New York: The Overlook Press, 2013). See also, Jacob Boas,

None passed muster with "Fabrizius." *Ruths schwere Stunde* (Ruth's difficult hour) was dismissed as "rather kitschy." Set against the bewildering political situation in Munich in 1919, the novel tells the story of a journalist who falls in love with a much older writer with whom she has a child out of wedlock. Though the book contained some excellent descriptions, Thelen observed, they fell short of redeeming it, while the use of attention-grabbing devices such as letter spacing and cursive type, the critic put down as a stylistic weakness.[10]

Rosenemil did not fare much better. A petty criminal in prewar Berlin, Rosenemil's occupational pursuits ran the gamut from hawking trashy novels, pimping, and burglary, to selling flowers. "Pleasant enough" and better than *Ruth schwere Stunde*, though the style once again disappointed, and the use of Berlin dialect was off-putting. "Not a bad book, just not my taste."[11]

Thelen reviewed *Der unbekannte Fussgänger* (The unknown pedestrian) and *Der Etruskische Spiegel* (The Etruscan mirror) on September 13, 1936.[12] The "unknown pedestrian" is Benno Meyer, a German-Jewish emigrant in Paris who dies attempting to extract a former lover from a burning vehicle. He goes to heaven where a higher court passes judgment. Thelen enjoyed the novel's beginning, Benno Meyer's thoughts and aperçus about the country and people, life and death, God and the devil – all of which helped offset the weak *deus ex machina* ending. "In Georg Hermann we have lost a gifted 'Baedeker.'"[13] The Baedeker metaphor crosses the Italian border, as does *Der Etruskische Spiegel*'s protagonist, an unmarried German-Jewish emigrant and

"Albert Vigoleis Thelen and Émigré Literature: Dispatches from Mallorca and Other European Venues, 1934–1940," in *Spanienbilder aus dem deutschsprachigen Exil bei Feuchtwanger und seinen Zeitgenossen*, Feuchtwanger Studies, Vol. 5, Isabel Hernández, ed. (Oxford, Bern, New York: Peter Lang, 2018), 323–338.

10. "Georg Hermann scheitert," *Het Vaderland*, July 22, 1934.

11. Ibid., December 8, 1935.

12. "Romane von Georg Hermann und Hermann Kesten. Ein Buch über Struensee." For the original German of Thelen's reviews "in den vreemde," see Albert Vigoleis Thelen, *Die Literatur in der Fremde: Literaturkritiken*, ed., trans. and with a foreword by Erhard Louven (Bonn: Weidle, 1966).

13. *Baedeker*, a popular travel guide.

architect *d'un certain age* named Harry Frank. "Hermann seems to be an expert on Rome, traversing Italy with open eyes and a warm heart, complemented by a natural appreciation of art objects." On his way to Rome, fleeing humiliation and hatred in the Third Reich, Harry hooks up with a beautiful Italian woman and gets hold of an Etruscan mirror that forecasts a horrific event. Harry loses his grip, chucks the mirror into the ocean, and drowns trying to bury it on the ocean floor. Thelen: "The book is rich in cutting observations, daring comparisons and wit, but here, too, the details gum up the narrative."

Reviewers cited by Hermann biographer (and great-grandson) John Craig-Sharples were decidedly more upbeat. Alfred Döblin found *Der unbekannte Fussgänger* "strange but interesting." *Der Etruskische Spiegel* found favor with Chris de Graaff of *Het Algemeen Handelsblad*, Hermann's former employer. "In this book," wrote De Graaff on March 7, 1936, "I especially enjoyed its calm, harmonious style and melancholy philosophizing, two qualities which distinguishes it from much of contemporary German literature, regardless of origin, inside or outside the Third Reich."[14] *Rosenemil* as well had its admirers. "In the meantime," Sigmund Freud wrote to Hermann, "I have read your *Rosenemil* and am still full of it, so full that I can scarcely praise the novel enough. And it displays your characteristic trademark. It contains a large slice of the strange magic of the dark side of Berlin."[15]

Craig-Sharples notes that in the first six months of 1936 his great-grandfather made all of six guilders, and that same year resorted to a handout from Amsterdam's Jewish Refugee Committee.[16]

In the second half of the 1930s, with Hitler firmly in command and no end to exile in sight, a different kind of Jew emerges in the works of Jewish authors published abroad. German-speaking Jews had turned out to be *toevallige Duitschers* – accidental Germans – after all, Thelen observed in September 1939. They appeared to have lost interest in the events inside Germany and were moving on. One direction in

---

14. Cited in John Craig-Sharples, *Georg Hermann: A Writer's Life* (Cambridge: Legenda, 2019), 218.

15. Ibid., 203.

16. Ibid., 218–219.

which they were moving was Palestine. Since 1933, Zionism had made significant inroads in the German-Jewish community. Hermann, however, was not interested in the creation of a Jewish homeland. He self-identified as a *Kulturjude*, a cultural Jew, neither Zionist nor religious. He believed that Zionism was a wrong turn in the road and one best not taken. "For Hermann, individual nation states, drenched in the idiocy of patriotism, are a construct which must be overcome."[17]

5. *Eine Zeit stirbt* – Death of an Era

"Overall," Hermann explains in a scene-setting foreword to *Eine Zeit stirbt* (1933) (Death of an era), the fifth and final installment in a chain of novels profiling the generation that came into the world between 1870 and 1880. For the most part, Hermann's generation consisted of well-off Berlin Jewish professionals, convinced that the Great Inflation of 1923 spelled the end of an era.[18]

Eine Zeit stirbt, Hermann's requiem for a generation, eerily circumscribes the arc of his own life, from his birth, the founding of the German Reich and full Jewish emancipation, both in 1871; the economic collapse of 1873/74, through the war years, postwar turmoil and the hyperinflation of 1923; the rise of Hitler, flight, poverty, deportation, and death in Auschwitz – in short, an era that started on a high note and ended in a death rattle.

Hermann's father's business went belly-up in 1876, a blow from which the Borchardts never recovered. Whether caused by the stock market crash of 1873 is unclear. Subsequently the Borchardts "moved home repeatedly...as they slid inexorably down the social pecking order."[19] The strainer effect of this crash, the elimination of unproductive enterprises and the concentration of economic clout in fewer hands, set the stage for Germany's economic miracle of the late nineteenth century. It also begot the so-called "social problem," the

---

17. Ibid., 246.
18. Hermann's pentalogy (1917–1934) includes *Einen Sommer lang; Kleinen Gast; November achtzehn; Ruths schwere Stunde, Eine Zeit stirbt*.
19. Craig-Sharples, *Hermann*, 17.

shorthand for low wages, unemployment, inadequate housing, and other ills associated with unchecked industrialization. And the even shorter hand of Jewish culpability.

Antisemitism found a receptive audience across class lines. In 1881, Chancellor Otto von Bismarck accepted a petition bearing 267,000 signatures entitled "The Emancipation of the German People from the Yoke of Jewish Rule." With the return of prosperity around the middle of the 1890's, the preoccupation with *Weltpolitik*, and the growing might of Social Democracy, the Jewish question faded in importance, so much so that in 1906 Social Democrat August Bebel declared antisemitism to have "no prospect whatsoever of ever exercising a decisive influence on political and social life in Germany."[20]

But despite setbacks, it was in Wilhelmine Germany that Jews laid the foundation for their not inconsiderable economic clout, even more remarkable because there were so few of them: roughly 500,000. From publishing to electrical works, and from banking to academia and politics, Jews made their presence felt. In the elections of 1912, twelve of the 110 Social Democratic Reichstag seats (out of 397) went to Jews. Enemies on the right took note, branding the election a *Judenwahl* – Jewish election – and the Reichstag a *Judenreichstag*. That same year, 1912, the literary critic Moritz Goldstein published an article in *Kunstwart*, Germany's leading cultural journal, that created quite a stir and was later quoted by Nazi works on German Jews. "We Jews," wrote Goldstein, "are administering the spiritual property of a nation which denies our right to do so." Forty-five years later, Goldstein recalled why he had written "Deutsch-Jüdischer Parnass." He was driven, he said, "by an irresistible urge to release the pressure which had accumulated in my mind. So I sat down to describe the position of the literary Jew in Germany as I saw it; to point out the intolerable and undignified ambiguity; to demonstrate the meaning of being a Jew and the impossibility of overcoming it."[21]

---

20. August Bebel famously defined antisemitism as "the socialism of fools."
21. Moritz Goldstein, "German Jewry's Dilemma. The Story of Provocative Essay," *Year Book of the Leo Baeck Institute*, Volume 2, Issue 1, January 1957, 237. In a letter to Max Brod, Franz Kafka acknowledged the validity of Karl

Nonetheless, the overwhelming majority of German Jews could not think of themselves as anything but German. Their *Deutschtum* ("Germanism") was something they had come to take for granted; sacred. Jews and non-Jews and Jews marched off to war to the beat of "The Song of Hate Against England," the wildly popular tune composed by the German-Jewish playwright and lyricist Ernst Lissauer. In August 1914, the Verband der deutschen Juden (Association of German Jews) urged Jews to volunteer for the war effort "over and above the call of duty." The appeal did not fall on deaf ears. 100,000 Jews saw military service of one kind or another; 35,000 earned distinguished service medals; 2,000 made officer, thousands died on the battlefield. A who's who of the German intelligentsia signed the October 1914 "Manifesto to the Civilized World," a statement disavowing German war guilt and justifying the invasion of neutral Belgium. Among its 93 signatories were five prominent Jews: munitions maven Fritz Haber; the Nobel Prize-winning biologist Paul Ehrlich; the legal scholar Paul Laband; the painter Max Liebermann, and the stage director and impresario Max Reinhardt.

Georg Hermann's name was not among the 93 signatories. Hermann was a pacifist. This placed him *hors de combat*, beyond the mainstream. "[O]nly a very small number of German writers did resist and keep their distance from the warmongers. Heinrich Mann was one, Georg Hermann another."[22] Much like Karl Kraus in Austria, Hermann wrote essays debunking the war effort. Craig-Sharples:

Hermann laments the way German intellectuals have embraced the war so indiscriminately and in so doing side-lined completely consideration of every other social ill. He argues persuasively (in a 1915 essay) that reducing poverty, improving public health, and making progress in areas such as agriculture and transportation,

Kraus' "diagnosis, suggesting that the adoption of German by Jewish writers is inescapably problematic." Edward Timms, *Karl Kraus, Apocalyptic Satirist: The Post-War Crisis and the Rise of the Swastika* (New Haven and London: Yale University Press, 2005), 244.
22. Craig-Sharples, *Hermann*, 78.

will be far more significant to mankind in the long run than transient shifts in the balance of political power.[23]

Two years into the war, the military prepared a census of Jews, the so-called *Judenzählung*, to determine the number of Jewish slackers, draft dodgers, war profiteers, and in the war agencies at home, which rumor put at astronomical heights. It found that by November 1, 1916, 3,411 Jewish bodies had been left behind on the battlefield, apparently meeting the War Minister's quota for dead Jews, for the report never saw the light of day until after the conflict.

For Jews like Hermann, the "Jewish Census" was the last straw, the end of the "assimilationist" dream, the much-vaunted German-Jewish symbiosis. World War I turned out to be a decisive turning-point, shattering the illusion of unlimited progress on every front. Gone was the prewar era exalted by Stefan Zweig and other beneficiaries of "the world of yesterday," superseded by an age Hermann Broch (1886–1951) conceptualized as "the disintegration of all values." "… [I]t is," the German novelist reflected in *The Sleepwalkers*, "as if the monstrous reality of the war had blotted out the reality of the world.…

> An age that is softer and more cowardly than any preceding age suffocates in waves of blood and poison gas; nations of bank clerks and profiteers hurl themselves upon barbed wire; a well-organized humanitarianism avails to hinder nothing, but calls itself the Red Cross and prepares artificial limbs for the victims; towns starve and coin money out of their own hunger; spectacled schoolteachers lead storm troops; city dwellers live in caves; factory hands and other civilians crawl out on reconnoitering duty, and in the end, once they are back in safety, apply their artificial limbs once more to the making of profits. Amid a blurring of all forms, in a twilight of apathetic uncertainly brooding over a ghostly world, man like a lost child gropes his way by the help of a small frail thread through a dream landscape that he calls reality and that is nothing but a nightmare to him.[24]

---

23. Ibid., 84.
24. *The Sleepwalkers*, trans. Willa and Edwin Muir (San Francisco: North Point Press, 1985), 373.

Win or lose, there was a price to be paid. But losers are losers, and there's nothing to celebrate; someone, or something, must be held accountable. There was much talk of Jews stabbing Germany in the back while the "unvanquished" army in the field was about to wrap up the victory; of a "Jewish Republic," a "Jewish press," and a "Jewish plot" to bury Germany under a revolutionary avalanche.

6. Georg Hermann's *J'Accuse*

In 1933, having settled in Holland and witnessed the assault on Jewish life east of the border – the April 1 boycott of Jewish businesses and services, and the non-Aryan legislation of April 7, 1933, banning Jews from the civil service, and additional efforts to leach Jews from the political, economic, and social life of the nation – Georg Hermann fired off *J'Accuse*, a searing, Zolaesque indictment of the German people.

> We, the German Jews, and Jews all over the world, reproach the German people that they did not act immediately when Hitler and his followers, ten and more years ago, took recourse to antisemitism in its vilest form, and turned it into a party platform in order to win over the musty and blockheaded peasantry, as well as the vapid middle classes to its political purposes."

Hermann's preamble launched a laundry list of accusations. A selection follows.

> When they began chant their slogan, 'Juda verrecke!' ("Jews perish!") in the streets...
> When they fantasized... about future pogroms...
> When "Jewish treason," "Jewish murder" and a thousand similar expressions desecrated the German language...
> When in the thousands of meetings paid for by the great landowners, captains of industry and other moneyed people, the most unbelievable libels against German Jews were uttered...
> When, with songs like "Wetzt die langen Messer auf dem Bürgersteig, lasst die Messer flutschen in den Judenleib" ("Sharpen the long knives on the sidewalk, let the knives slip into the Jew's body") they fantasized about future pogroms.

As Jews we feel insulted, vituperated, hindered, endangered, limited in breathing life's air and in life's sphere. All this we could bear. The history of Jewry has taught us to bear and overcome such things without impairing our human dignity. But as Germans we are ashamed – and this is the worst – as every decent German now ought to be ashamed, ought to have been ashamed from the hour that the earth over the graves of our young Jewish brothers in Flanders, in Russia, on the slopes of the Alps, in the Vosges, in the Balkans and in the Sinai, had not yet dried, that the stumps of young Jewish brothers, had not yet healed in their bandages and even then the hydra of blind Jew-hatred had raised its poisonous, horrible head, which ought not only to have been cut off but which should have immediately been burned to the very roots.

But our severest reproach against the sixty million fellow Germans who did not take part in that agitation and were not caught, befuddled, and robbed of their judgement by the same, is that they did not cry out with sixty million voices:

We do not suffer in our country such a crime against civilisation! To a man we denounce this campaign of hate! We denounce these forgers of lies. We declare that antisemitism in whatever form, is not worthy of Germany! And we are ashamed that it leads to such revolting excesses! We declare that our fellow Jewish countryman who for almost twenty centuries has resided in this land, has done his duty to the state as well as anyone, and therefore enjoys the same rights as we do, and should be protected against slander and discrimination in the state – and we declare that we should protect him with the complete power of the machinery of the state against vilification and against the incitement of the base instincts of the rabble by those without conscience, the architects of Germany's grave.

… That an end shall be made to antisemitism, of this disgrace to civilization which has assumed the most despicable form.… That the government itself put a stop to it, even if it did sow the wind, in order to reap the storm.[25]

---

25. Cited in Craig-Sharples, *Hermann*, 168–172.

7. Last Years

Georg Hermann wasn't happy in the Netherlands. Provincial. He missed Berlin. "In March [1933]," he wrote in 1938, "I turned my back on my beloved fatherland and went on with my life in Holland, where it pretty much proceeds as before, except, possibly, somewhat lonelier than in Neckärgemund near Heidelberg, where I lived during the final, German years."[26]

Georg Borchardt's Family Card furnishes the details of his card-self. Date and city and country of birth (box 4). Nationality, Box 5: Vr = *Vreemdeling*, i.e., alien. (7) Interestingly, his profession, "writer," has been crossed out and replaced by "zonder," "without." Box 8 records

---

26. https://www.joodsmonument.nl/nl/page/381828/georg-hermann
-borchardt-autobiografisch.

the names of his parents; 9 through 16 contains information about his first wife, Lotte Samter, date of birth and death. Box 21 gives Hermann's Amsterdam address as Jekerstraaat 71-II and his internment in Westerbork as September 1, 1943 (boxes 21, 22).[27] Box 27 records the date of marriage of Hermann's daughter, Ursula Henriette, to J.H. Kalmann, September 18, 1940, and states that [Herbert] Kalmann departed for Great Britain on January 15, 1941. The marriage was short-lived; Herbert never set foot in Westerbork. "Lisa" is Hermann's daughter "Elise" ("Liese") (Box 28); Elise and Hermann's former wife, Martha Heynemann fled to England in the nick of time. Top center: date and place of death, Auschwitz, November 19, 1943, added after the war.

By 1941, authority over Jewish affairs in Berlin had been vested in the Jewish Department of Heydrich's Security Service, Section IVB4, headed, in 1942, by Adolf Eichmann. A branch of IVB4, the euphemistically designated Central Office for Jewish Emigration, began operating in Holland in September 1941. Subsequently, a plethora of decrees washed over Jews like a tidal wave, separating them out from the non-Jewish population and facilitating their destruction. In April 1943, all Jews in the provinces were ordered to report to Camp Vught, the labor and internment camp in the south of Holland.[28] Two weeks later, the "Final Solution" entered its final phase.

"In January 1943," recalled Hermann's daughter Ursula (Usche) after the war (writing in English),

> a German officer came to our place (in Hilversum). He was not at all interested in Peps [Hermann], the author, but had heard that we possessed a large art collection. The officer was friendly and had a good look around at what was in the flat. He was obviously visualizing what would look good in his villa. Peps being naïve was so attached to his things, that, even when we had no money and he might at least have sold some things, he never did so. This would have helped us a lot, because with just a few things sold, there was

---

27. The actual date of his internment in Westerbork is June 20, 1943. Wartime entries on Jews' Family Cards often are hit and miss.
28. It doesn't appear that Hermann went to Vught.

still a huge amount left. The whole flat was just crammed full with art objects. Before leaving, the German officer said, "You will move out within forty-eight hours." Peps said. "What will happen to the things in the apartment?" and the officer said "Don't worry, they are valuable so they will be taken good care of." Again Peps' naivete revealed itself. I recall that during that forty-eight-hour period, I used the baby stroller in the evening and made trips to Elsje (de Groot) and to other people, in order to hide them. I already understood that I had to do this otherwise all would have been lost.[29]

No doubt, the remainder of Hermann's collection of books and artifacts, crated and slated for Germany at the behest of Task Force Rosenberg, was headed for the homes of Nazi *Bonzen* or museums, including, one would think, copies of Hermann's novels consigned to the flames as "un-German" in the literary auto-da-fe of May 10, 1933.

On June 20, 1943, the Germans launched a round-the-clock raid, ensnaring a thousand Amsterdam Jews. The catch included Hermann, his daughter Ursula (Usche) and her son Micky. Trams transported them to Amsterdam's Central Station, where they were loaded onto cattle cars and deported to Westerbork.

Ursula wrote that the camp "was basically okay, but every now and again people committed suicide by hanging themselves, especially just before transportations were due."[30]

Westerbork diarist Philip Mechanicus noted that "[t]he old literary man, Georg Hermann, the author of *Jettchen Gebert* walks around as stiff as a door, but in beach wear with a cap and a walking stick and asks everyone: 'Well, my friend, what's new? You know so much.' And tells jovial jokes, as in *Jettchen.*"[31] Small children in the camp called him "opa" – grandfather.[32]

---

29. Ursula Borchardt (Shulamit BenDror in Israel), cited in Craig-Sharples *Georg Hermann*, 261–262. Interned in Transit Camp Westerbork in 1943, Ursula, managed to obtain Palestine Certificates for herself and little boy, Micky (Miki Ben-Dror in Israel).

30. Cited in Craig-Sharples, *Hermann*, 264.

31. Philip Mechanicus, cited in Craig-Sharples, *Hermann*, 265.

32. https://www.joodsmonument.nl/nl/page/515596/about-georg-borchardt.

Amsterdam's Jewish Council kept track of Hermann's dimming existential prospects. His cards[33] indicate that Prisoner 51104 arrived in Westerbork on June 20, 1943, housed in Barrack 55; daughter Ursula and grandson Micky (March 13, 1941) in 57. The cards further indicate that the seventy-one-year-old diabetic and heart patient explored several channels to secure his release. On the 27th, the Jewish Council took note of a request to have him transferred to a castle repurposed to accommodate "meritorious Jewish nationals." On the 29th, the Jewish Council observed that as a *Buitenlander* ("foreigner") Hermann's prospects were slim. On July 3, the Council's Emigration Department acknowledged that "Borchardt" often went by "Georg Hermann." An application for a Palestine Certificate, based on his contribution to German literature, also came a cropper. Hermann was, however, found eligible to receive a monthly stipend from the Borchardt-Cohen Foundation Schaffhausen. Family in Switzerland eventually managed to secure Palestine Certificates for Ursula and her son, Micky.

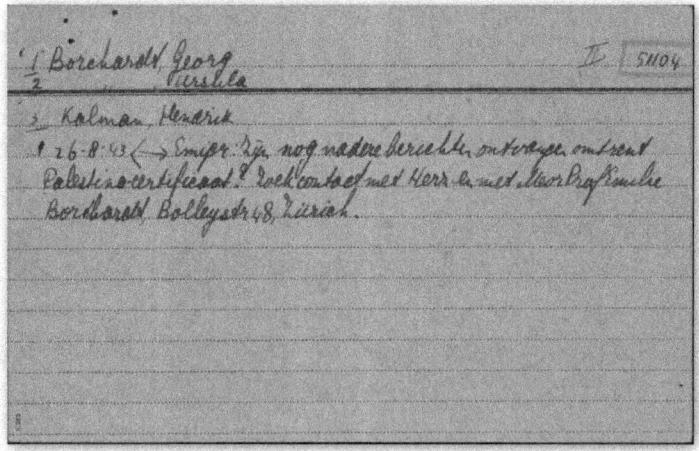

By this time, close to 89,000 Jews had been deported "to the East."

Evidence suggests that Hermann, given the state of his health and psyche, pursued his release half-heartedly, rejecting a Paraguayan

---

33. Jewish Council cards, Camp Westerbork archive.

passport that acquaintances had contrived to secure. All attempts to stave off the inevitable having come up short, Hermann was deported to Auschwitz on November 16, 1943, and gassed upon arrival.

The *Auschwitz Chronicle* records that on November 17, 1943, "995 Jews arrive from Westerbork in an RSHA transport from Holland. In the transport are 166 children, 281 men and 291 women below the age of 50, and 257 old people.[34] After the selection, 275 men and 189 women are admitted to the camp and receive Nos. 163798–164072 and 68724–68912. The remaining 531 people are killed in the gas chambers."[35]

Survivor Lex van Weren:

I was deported on November 16.... In our wagon was Rabbi Dasberg from Utrecht, who sang and prayed on the way. We knew that we were going to Poland. Luckily, not Mauthausen, I thought, because all that came back from there were death notices. All those men who had been rounded up in Amsterdam just before the February strike went to Mauthausen.

Now and then the train stopped, doors opened. Grüne Polizei carried out the looting. We had to hand over all our money, our watches, fountain pens, and more. Most of our valuable possessions had already been taken from us by Lippmann-Rosenthal[36] in Westerbork. You were beaten if the Grüne Polizei didn't collect enough. This happened about five, six times during the trip.... In Dresden we stopped for ten hours; it had just been bombed. That

---

34. RSHA = Reichssicherheitsdienst, SS security force.

35. Danuta Czech, *Auschwitz Chronicle 1939–1945* (New York: An Owl Book Henry Holt and Company, 1997), 528–29. The train consisted of 27 cars, 995 deportees, including 228 children, and arrived on November 19. Luijters, *In Memoriam*, 693.

36. The graphic documenting transport activity in *De Jaren '40–'45* (The '40s and 50s), Rijksinstituut voor oorlogsdocumentatie (Netherlands Institute for War Documentation), 1961, 142. The book documents the war years through original sources, photographs, drawings, and newspaper clippings. Lippmann-Rosenthal, despite its Jew-sounding name a German looting bank associated with Alfred Rosenberg's Task Force.

was tough. In a freight car like that you had to either try to sit or lie helter-skelter across one another.… That literally all Jews were going to be murdered didn't ever cross our minds, did it? I was told this upon arrival in Auschwitz and didn't want to believe it. It was beyond my capacity to grasp it…As soon as the doors opened, I knew all was lost. It was the first time I experienced a feeling like that. Our lives were in immediate danger. We sensed that. At first it was dead quiet. Then, suddenly, incessant shouting, a chorus of men screaming *"raus…raus…raus"* ["Out! Out! Out!"]. They beat us with sticks and whips. All I could do was look at the faces of the SS-men. Terrifying! Later it turned out that this was a special *Kommando*.

Foggy, misty weather. Very early in the morning, on the cusp between night and day, from dark to light. It was as though it wasn't me experiencing it. An uncanny sensation. It subsequently dawned on me that the SS waited expressly to open up the wagons until the passage from night to day; pale twilight, wisps of mist. A good fit for the macabre SS ritual.… Then, suddenly, you were walking past an SS-man whose gloved hand pointed left, right, left, right. Left: you went to the trucks that drove straight to the gas chambers, although you didn't of course know this at the time. Right: you were allowed to go to another row granting life.… The people in The Canada-Detail[37] told us, "Say that you're healthy!" And to the mothers with children, "Get rid of your children! Give them to an older woman." But where's the mother capable of doing that? Five, perhaps ten minutes earlier you still had ideals, hope, expectations, fantasies.[38]

8. *Das gibt's nur einmal – It only happens once*

Plantage Middenlaan 42. Amsterdam's Jewish Theater.

---

37. Canada Detail (Kanada-Kommando), a Jewish detail tasked with sifting through the belongings of new arrivals.
38. Lex van Weren, "trompettist in Auschwitz," one of 16 male survivors. Dick Walda, *Trompettist in Auschwitz. Herinneringen van Lex van Weren*, cited in Luijters, *In Memoriam*, 693–694.

Starting in October 1941, this was a Jews-only theater. The building had 900 seats. Here one could listen to the Jewish symphony orchestra, which included many musicians terminated by the Concertgebouw Orchestra. They were only allowed to perform works by Jewish composers. The Jewish Chamber Orchestra, the Jewish Popular Orchestra and the Jewish Cabaret Ensemble ... also performed here.... From the end of June 1942 there were only afternoon performances because Jews had to stay home between 8:00 in the evening until 6:00 in the morning. The theater served as a venue for marriages when Jews were no longer allowed to get married at city hall. The final performance, Ladislas Fodor's comedy *Wiegelied* [Lullaby] took place on Sunday afternoon, July 19, 1942. The next day, the theater became a holding pen for thousands of Jews.[39]

One of the theater's first shows had been "Hand in Hand," a cabaret staged in the fall of 1941 starring uprooted German-Jewish performers and popular local entertainers. Towards the end, Kurt Gerron[40] sang "Das gibt's nur einmal, das kommt nicht wieder," the nine-minute ode to happiness from *Der Kongress tanzt*, the 1931 film starring Lilian Harvey. "With every refrain," recalled Herbert Scherzer, a German-Jewish actor and entertainer, "more and more handkerchiefs appeared, until there wasn't a dry eye in the house."[41]

Das gibt's nur einmal, das kommt nicht wieder,
das ist zu schön um wahr zu sein.
So wie ein Wunder fällt auf uns nieder
vom Paradies ein gold'ner Schein.
Das gibt's nur einmal, das kommt nicht wieder,

das ist vielleicht nur Träumerei.
Das kann das Leben nur einmal geben,

---

39. Bianca Stigter, *Atlas van een bezette stad: Amsterdam, 1940–1945* (Atlas of an occupied city) (Amsterdam: Atlas Contact, 2019), 225–226.
40. See, Chapter 1, fn. 1.
41. "Kabarett in Amsterdam während des Zweiten Weltkriegs. *Aufbau*, August 28, 1987.

vielleicht ist's morgen schon vorbei.
Das kann das Leben nur einmal geben,
denn jeder Frühling hat nur einen Mai.

It happens only once,
only once.
Too beautiful
to be true.
Like a miracle
a golden glow from paradise
shining down upon us.

It happens only once,
only once.
Perhaps it's but a dream,
a once in a lifetime dream
that may be over by tomorrow.
It only happens once,
once in a lifetime,
for every Spring has only one May.[42]

The last transport from the Jewish Theater took place on the day Georg Hermann was murdered in Auschwitz, November 19, 1943.

* * *

---

42. https://www.youtube.com>watch?v=MtxuPxAUQLo (accessed April 2, 2022).

Chapter III

Franz Müller and the White Rose

All of humanity's problems stem from man's inability to sit quietly in a room alone.   – Blaise Pascal

1. Wedontdothat

Well might Pascal contend that most of the world's problems are caused by those unwilling to stay put in their room, it is no less true that there always have been, and always will be, those who get off the couch, quit the room, lock the door, and go forth to confront evil. Take Günther Grass's "Wedontdothat." In *Peeling the Onion* (2008), Germany's Nobel Prize-winning novelist disclosed that at 17 he had served in the Waffen SS, the military arm of the SS. After 60 years posing as Germany's chief town crier, pillorying the nation for its wartime crimes, finger-pointing his way to literary fame and fortune, the aged German novelist had at last come clean. Sparing no one, young or old, Grass raised the specter of complicity. Youth, he said, is no excuse. "[W]e let ourselves, I let myself, be seduced."

"Wedontdothat" was the exception. Grass' fellow recruit said NO, deflecting every attempt to turn him into a *Mitlaufer* – "follower" – with the phrase "we don't do that," clinging to his credo with the same obstinacy Melville's Bartleby clung to "I would prefer not to" when asked to perform some odious piece of office business. The youthful

Hitlerites, Grass recalled, hated him for it, beat him, and urinated on his straw pallet. In the end, though, "Wedontdothat" "transformed us," and was sorely missed when he was dispatched to a concentration camp. Even so, "[h]e did not, become a role model."

SCHOOL FOR BARBARIANS

"Give me the youth and I have the future," Hitler declared. The Führer envisioned raising a youthful elite "before which the world would shrink back": violent, brutal, intrepid, indifferent to pain, pitiless, "hard as Krupp Steel," "a beast of prey."

In his review of Erika Mann's *Zehn Millionen Kinder* (1938), an account of the state of education under National Socialism, Dutch cultural critic Menno ter Braak pondered: "How will a youth raised in a harsh and suggestive monolithic ideology respond? Will it go into opposition at a critical juncture, or will it become the most ardent supporter of the system?... On the one hand, the purely biological fact of being young separates youth from their educators and tends to subject the system of these educators to criticism; on the other, the Nazi educational system is an undisputed *novum* in European history.... Indoctrination is a basic principle of the Nazi program."

They are betting on the young people, drilled in school and the Hitler Youth, to become standard bearers of a single worldview. It's not so much the information being provided that determines the totality of this drilling but its deliberate and systematic suppression. This is how critical awareness is neutered. Without recourse to information other than that provided by official channels, criticism becomes...a vague frustrated feeling incapable of coalescing into an alternate world view.... Are the traditions of that former Germany slated to vanish altogether or is there enough of a reservoir passed down by the older generations which may yet turn out to be sufficiently robust to allow for further development? We don't know and don't care to speculate about the future. The best we can do, as we await future developments, is to record and to continue to hope.[1]

---

1. Menno ter Braak, *Cultural Criticism in the Netherlands, 1933–1940: The*

Which, despite all attempts to channel education into physical activity and reducing intellectual life to a minimum, notes the reviewer, is the upshot of Erika Mann's book.

2. Franz Müller – The White Rose's *J'Accuse!*

Dinner with Franz Müller in a Munich restaurant was a whistlestop on the "Information Tour for Representatives of Holocaust Memorials USA." Organized by the Federal Republic of Germany on the 50th anniversary of the end of the war, our party of six consisted of four survivors, one spouse, and a guide from a government agency tasked with chaperoning us during the two-week visit to the land of our murderers. Munich saw the beginnings of the Hitler movement, its capital. Twenty kilometers to the northwest lies Dachau, Germany's first concentration camp, operational within months of Hitler's advent to power, which we had visited the previous day. With the memorial site still fresh in our mind, we sat down with 71-year-old Mr. Müller. In March of 1943, Mr. Müller had been arrested by the Gestapo for distributing the sixth and last pamphlet of the anti-Nazi White Rose Society. The previous February, two of the society's principals, Hans and Sophie Scholl, had been apprehended distributing flyers at Munich University. Convening four days after their arrest on February 18, the "People's Court," presided over by Nazi ideologist Roland Freisler, found:

> That the accused have in time of war by means of leaflets called for the sabotage of the war effort and armaments and for the overthrow of the National Socialist way of life of our people, have propagated defeatist ideas, and have most vulgarly defamed the Fuhrer, thereby giving aid to the enemy of the Reich and weakening the armed security of the nation. On this account they are

---

Newspaper Columns of Menno ter Braak. Introduced, edited and translated by Jacob Boas (Leiden/Boston: Brill/Rodopi, 2020), 210–12. Erika Mann *Zehn millionen Kinder: Die Erziehung der Jugend im Dritten Reich* (Amsterdam: Querido Verlag, 1938) (*School for Barbarians: Education under the Nazis* (New York: Dover Publications, 2014).

to be punished by *Death* [italics in the original]. Their honor and rights as citizens are forfeited for all time.

This was the method of *Volksrecht*, the "People's Law." There were no defense attorneys, the verdicts a foregone conclusion. Hans and Sophie Scholl were hanged that same day, as was Christoph Probst. "Co-conspirators" Alexander Schmorell, Kurt Huber, and Willi Graf, and Hans Leipelt were hanged in July and October; Hans Leipelt in January 1945. Huber, a teacher of philosophy at the University of Munich, was fifty years old. The other victims were in their early to mid-twenties twenties.

Franz Müller was arrested in April 1943. Because of his youth – he was eighteen – and his appearance – blond and eyes of blue – Franz lived up to the Aryan ideal, mystifying the prosecution. Labeling Franz and Franz's former classmate Hans Hirzel as "immature boys misled by enemies of the state,"[2] the prosecution sentenced both to five years imprisonment. Between 1943 and 1945, Müller was in and out of seven prisons. Trained as a corpsman, he nursed anti-Nazi prisoners and slept well, he told student interviewers in 2011.[3] Liberated by American soldiers, he walked back home to Ulm, covering 40 km on foot. He next went on to study law, he said, because the Nazis had destroyed it. Freedom, peace, and human rights, he added, comprised the essence of the message propagated by the White Rose.

3. Youth Without God

Franz Josef Müller grew up in Ulm. This was fortunate. Ulm wasn't Munich. The school he attended, a humanist-oriented gymnasium, was not Nazi, though the principal was. Franz recalled having to translate Plato's dialogues from ancient Greek. The discussion centered on whether it was better to suffer injustice than to commit it. "This was a

---

2. https://libcom.org/library/white-rose-sentencing-transcripts (accessed November 10, 2022).
3. "Interview mit Herrn Franz Müller, 29.09.2011."
https://edisciplinas.usp.br/pluginfile.php/256444/course/section/78106/anotacoes-mueller.pdf (accessed November 10, 2022).

roundabout way of confronting Nazi ideology," Müller told Christoph Lindenmeyer on Bavarian radio on May 2, 2003.[4] As well, he recalled, at the gymnasium Catholics and Protestants came together, helping erase differences. A White Father priest was instrumental in organizing a group of like-minded students. Weekly, some 20 to 24 students would meet at the Roman Catholic missionary's house to mull things over, at the conclusion of which they might find Hitler Youth waiting to trounce them. In 2003, Franz was still amazed that the Gestapo left them alone. Then again, the Gestapo in Ulm wasn't all that bad and informers sparse, he said.

Asked about his home life, Müller said that his family was Catholic, his mother a "born anti-Nazi," his father pro, joining the party in 1933, a "fellow traveler," albeit with reservations. Catholics, too, professed to have the truth, and occasionally Nazi youths turned up at the church baiting youthful attendees to dump the Mass and join their ranks instead.

There is no telling whether Franz Müller or any of his White Rose cohorts had read Ödön von Horváth's 1937 novel *Jugend ohne Gott (Youth without God)*.[5] Horváth's novel was banned in Germany shortly after its publication in Amsterdam in 1937.[6] *Jugend ohne Gott*, a fictionalized account of Erika Mann's "school for barbarians," covers some of the same ground as the White Rose leaflets. The "hero" is a nameless teacher "with a safe job and a pension at the end of the line." As the sole adult committed to speaking the truth, the teacher inspires the formation of a club that reads "everything that is forbidden ... and discuss how things ought to be in the world."

The problematic of resistance, free will, fence-sitting, God and godlessness, and the humanity of "non-Aryan" races are among the

---

4. https://www.br.de/fernsehen/ard-alpha/sendungen/alpha-forum/franz -josef-mueller-gespraech100.html (accessed November 10, 2022).

5. German text at www.literaturdownload.at/ Horvath.html (accessed October 29, 2022). English edition, *Youth Without God*, trans. R. Wills Thomas (New York: Neversink/Penguin Random House, 2012).

6. In 1933, von Horváth quit Germany for Austria, immigrated to Paris in 1938 and died that same year, felled by a branch from a tree during a thunderstorm.

issues von Horváth addresses in this slim, layered narrative. It is the racial dynamic, however, broached in the first of the novel's 44 brief chapters, that holds down the center. Defending the humanity of "the Negro," and by extension that of the Jews and other peoples at risk, had earned the teacher the derogatory sobriquet "Der Neger." Interestingly, in the novel a White Father comes to the rescue of the "compromised" teacher with an offer of a teaching position with the African-based Roman Catholic missionary society, with no strings attached.

"Those of us who have personal memories of a German school," recalled Albert Vigoleis Thelen in 1938,

> long before Hitler will find much in it that is vicious and a prepa-
> ration for a great abuse of power as that currently on offer. At the
> time of the war, citing the suffering of the men at the front, they
> drilled us among large, stinging nettles. But all this is mere child's
> play compared to the documentation furnished by the Ödön von
> Horváth novel *Jugend ohne Gott*, which focuses on the education
> of youth in a totalitarian state, with military desensitization its
> most important pedagogical component.[7]

Franz entered the Hitler youth in 1938, aged 14. His parents didn't discourage him. It was in the Hitler Youth, he told Christoph Linden-meyer, that he first encountered anti-Nazi views. "For me it wasn't like Mr. Scholl [Hans], who initially enjoyed being a Hitler Youth leader." Christoph Lindenmeyer: "So by then you were already re-sisting." Franz Müller: "That's saying a bit much. We were looking for ways out."

Outsiders were subject to peer pressure and discrimination, such as barring university enrollment and other career-threatening imped-iments. Not until 1939 was membership, open to boys 14 to 18, made compulsory. Boys learned how to shoot and scream "Jawohl!!" Discus-sion was out of the question. "Better left to horses since they had big-ger craniums," the saying went. The junior section of the Hitler Youth, known as *Pimpfs*, enrolled boys between 10 and 14. The boys' organi-zations preyed on young people's malleability and idealism, bound-

---

7. Albert Vigoleis Thelen, *Literatur in der Fremde*, May 15, 1938, 186.

less energy, thirst for adventure, or simply a break from home. The corresponding girls' organizations, *Bund Deutscher Mädel* and *Jungmädel*, groomed their charges for childbearing and domestic routines, encapsulated in the infamous three K's: *Kinder, Küche, Kirche*: "Children, Kitchen, Church."

4. "We Are Your Guilty Conscience" – the White Rose Pamphlets

By the time the White Rose started writing and distributing their leaflets in the summer of 1942, Franz was 17 going on 18. At 18, he was obliged to serve three to six months in the Reich Labor Service. The evening before his departure, friends came over and uncorked a bottle of wine, their first ever, and things got a little weird. His friend Hans Hirzel, the same who received a five-year prison term with Franz, handed him a White Rose pamphlet and asked him to read it. That brought him back to earth. "*Sprengstoff* [dynamite] – a death sentence if caught." Would he help disseminate it? Given his imminent departure, Franz declined, but left the door open.

It is not clear which of the four leaflets Franz read.[8] Say it was the first. "Nothing," the leaflet started out, "is so unworthy of a civilized nation as allowing itself to be 'governed' without

---

8. All six pamphlets, in English, at http://www.historyisaweapon.com /defcon1/whiterose.html.

opposition by an irresponsible clique that has yielded to base instinct. It is certain that today every honest German is ashamed of his government. Who among us has any conception of the dimensions of shame that will befall us and our children one day the veil has fallen from our eyes and the most horrible crimes – crimes that infinitely outdistance every human measure – reach the light of day?

Shades of Georg Hermann's *J'Accuse.*

The leaflet went on to remind their compatriots that by abandoning the will to take decisive action, they were sacrificing "their highest principle," that of free will. "If they are so devoid of all individuality, have already gone so far along the road toward turning into a spiritless and cowardly mass – then, yes, they deserve their downfall." And all that, including death on battlefield "for the hubris of a sub-human,... an insatiable demon." It was not too late, however, to fight back and "offer "passive resistance – *resistance* – wherever you may be, [and] forestall the spread of this atheistic war machine before it is too late."

To rouse the Germans from their stupor and complicity, in this and the remaining leaflets, the White Rose pushed a mix of literary, religious, philosophical, psychological, and historical buttons. Guilt-tripping, holding out the carrot of redemption and the stick of damnation, they named and shamed, invoking Schiller and Goethe, the avatars of a nation of "poets and thinkers"; Lao-Tze, Aristotle, Novalis, and Christian texts. Above all, they advocated passive resistance, as any other form was out of the question. Such resistance, they suggested, might include sabotage in the armaments industries; disrupting Nazi-Party public gatherings; refusal to contribute to public drives, "collections of metal, textiles, and the like," and convincing acquaintances, "including those in the lower social classes, of the senselessness of continuing, of the hopelessness of this war."

Each leaflet terminated with an appeal to "make as many copies as possible and distribute them." White Rose cohorts also plastered Munich's walls with slogans such as *Down with Hitler!* and *Freedom!*

The second leaflet cited the "cancerous growth" afflicting the entire body, silencing opponents. "The German intellectuals fled to their cellars, ... gradually to choke to death." A "wave of unrest," it said, was "go[ing] through the land" and urged people "to root out the brown horde" and be "cleansed by suffering." "After all, an end in terror is preferable to terror without end." Significantly, the leaflet also touched on the fate of the Jews. We do not want to discuss here the question of the Jews," the pamphlet declared, "nor do we want to compose a defense or apology.

> No, only by way of example do we want to cite the fact that since the conquest of Poland three hundred thousand Jews have been murdered in this country in the most bestial way. Here we see the most frightful crime against Jewish dignity, a crime that is unparalleled in the whole of history. For Jews, too, are human beings – no matter what position we take with respect to the Jewish question – and a crime of this dimension has been perpetrated against human beings.

"Someone may say," the pamphlet proceeded,

> that the Jews deserved their fate. This assertion would be a monstrous impertinence. ... Well, then, what about the Poles? Did they deserve their fate? ... [T]he fact that the entire Polish aristocratic youth is being annihilated? Concentration camps and forced labor for the male scions of the houses of the nobility between fifteen and twenty, and the girls of this age sent to Norway into the bordellos of the SS! Why tell you these things, since you are fully aware of them – or if not of these, then of other equally grave crimes committed by this frightful sub-humanity.

It was a shrewd move not to get bogged down in the Jewish question, seeing how much of the poison had penetrated all layers of society, while putting paid to the postwar *Davon haben wir nights gewusst!* – "We knew nothing about this!," i.e., the slaughter of the Jews.

"Jews, too, are human beings." It is quite likely that the phrasing harked back to Goebbels' November 16, 1941, radio address and article *Die Juden sind schuld!* – "The Jews Are to Blame!" In it, Goebbels took aim at those who sympathized with the Jews following September's introduction of the yellow star. Tokens of support included, in Goebbels' words, "parading down the Kurfürstendamm [Berlin's Champs d'Elysée] with them! Every Jew is a decent Jew who had found a dumb and ignorant goy [non-Jew] who thinks him decent!" "The excuse they give for their provocative conduct," the Minister of Propaganda declared, "is always the same: The Jews, too, after all are human beings, too. We never denied that… but so are murderers, child rapists, thieves, and pimps." It is the duty, he declared, of every German to support the state's anti-Jewish measures, including the introduction of the "Yellow Star," and that every person who defended the Jews deserved to be treated like one, "a craven coward" and "enemy agent.… For Jews started the war, masterminded it, and were responsible "for every fallen soldier."[9]

The third and fourth pamphlets hammered away at themes explored in the earlier ones, juxtaposing the Hell created by the Evil One, "the messengers of the Anti-Christ," with St. Augustine's *Civitas Dei* as "the model which the state should approximate," exhorting the apathetic, the slackers, lackeys, cowards, the hesitant and indifferent to get out of their rooms and make their way back to God. "For, according to God's will, man is intended to pursue his natural goal, his earthly happiness, in self-reliance and self-chosen activity, freely and independently within the community of life and work of the nation," and openly called for the military defeat of National Socialism and "a revival of the deeply wounded German spirit from within," a "rebirth… preceded by a clear confession of all the guilt the German has incurred and by a ruthless battle against Hitler and his all too many minions, Party members, Quislings, and the like."

---

9. Joachim Remak, ed. *The Nazi Years: A Documentary History* (Prospect Heights, Illinois: Waveland Press, 1990), 155–57. This was neither the first nor the last time Goebbels derided those who considered Jews human. "He is human, yes – but what kind? If someone hits your mother with a whip in the face, do you then also say: 'Thanks so much, he's human, too'?" That is not a human being but a brute." "Warum sind wir Judengegner" ("Why we are againt the Jews"), in *Der Angriff*, July 30, 1928. *Aufsätze aus der Kampfzeit* (München: Franz Eher Nachfolger, 1935), 329–332. https://ghdi.ghi-dc.org/docpage.cfm?docpage_id=5905&language=german (accessed November 3, 2022).

The first four pamphlets were produced by Hans Scholl and Alexander Morell, medical students at Munich University, prior to being sent to the Eastern Front. That experience shocked them so deeply that upon their return to Munich they drew up a fifth flyer. It was this flyer, the "most important," according to Müller, and the cause of his arrest, that he had typed up on his father's typewriter and helped distribute.[10] The flyer, also called the "European Flyer," described a Europe freed from the Nazi scourge.[11] Produced around the time of Germany's defeat at Stalingrad (February 1943), a turning point acknowledged in the opening line: "The war is approaching its destined end.... [I]n the east the armies are constantly in retreat and invasion imminent in the West. Mobilization in the US has not yet reached its climax.... But the Germans won't see and listen."

By now, the fate of the Jews was an open secret and the writing on the wall for all to see.

> Germans! Do you and your children want to suffer the same fate that befell the Jews? Do you want to be judged by the same standards as your traducers? Are we to be forever a nation which is hated and rejected by all mankind? No. Dissociate yourselves from National Socialist gangsterism. Prove by your deeds that you think otherwise. A new war of liberation is about to begin. The better part of the nation will fight on our side. Cast off the cloak of indifference you have wrapped around you. Make the decision before it is too late. Do not believe the National Socialist propaganda which has driven the fear of Bolshevism into your bones. Do not believe that Germany's welfare is linked to the victory of National Socialism for good or ill. A criminal regime cannot achieve a German victory. Separate yourselves in time from everything connected with National Socialism. In the aftermath a terrible but just judgment will be meted out to those who stayed in hiding, who were cowardly and hesitant.... Freedom of speech, freedom of religion, the protection of individual citizens from the

---

10. *Interview mit Herrn Franz Müller,* 29.09.2011. https://edisciplinas.usp.br /pluginfile.php/256444/course/section/78106/anotacoes-mueller.pdf
11. Ibid.

arbitrary will of criminal regimes of violence –these will be the bases of the New Europe.

The sixth and final leaflet, produced around the same time, brought about the Society's downfall. It mentioned the loss of 330,000 men at Stalingrad. "The frightful bloodbath has opened the eyes of even the stupidest German." The leaflet called upon students to get out of the lecture rooms of "party bootlickers," put an end to the "lewd jokes by Gauleiters"[12] targeting female students and rise up. In addition, the leaflet demanded Germany's unconditional surrender, as stipulated by the Allies at the Casablanca Conference the previous January. "Today Germany is as encircled as Stalingrad was. Hitler and his regime must fall so that Germany may live."

5. Franz Müller in Oregon

In 1986, determined to keep the legacy of the White Rose Society alive, Mr. Müller started the White Rose Foundation. A key component of that legacy is an exhibit at Munich University, the site of the Society's betrayal. At the time Mr. Müller and I hooked up, I was about to step into a job with the Holocaust Center at Oregon's Pacific University and invited him to bring the exhibit to its campus. Accordingly, in the late fall of 1995 Franz and his wife, Britta, stayed with us for a week. Mr. Müller fell in love with Oregon's wines, draining bottle after bottle, with more than a little help from his host. One fine day we drove to the coast. I don't remember the exact details but Franz and I, and perhaps Britta as well, went for a long walk on the beach – too long for the then 72-year-old. Would I get the car to get him? I said cars were strictly prohibited on this stretch. Franz looked at me with surprise – stuck on the rules?

The White Rose exhibit, hosted in the fall of 1995 by the Oregon Holocaust Resource Center at Pacific University in Forest Grove, attracted wide interest. High school students were bused from surrounding school districts. The exhibit featured photographs alternating with

---

12. Gauleiters, regional Nazi leaders

selections from the six pamphlets. Ancillary programming included Michael Verhoeven's film *The White Rose*[13] and an evening featuring a debate pitting Daniel Goldhagen's *Hitler's Willing Executioners: Ordinary Germans and The Holocaust* against Christopher Browning's *Ordinary Men: Reserve Police Battalion 101 and the Final Solution in Poland*. Neither author was present. Held in the university's main auditorium, participants included Franz Müller and two of the university's professors with an interest in Holocaust history and literature. I served as moderator.

By and large relying on the same data – an analysis of a German reserve police battalion ordered to kill 1,500 Jewish men, women, and children in Poland – political scientist Goldhagen, the son of Holocaust survivors, argued that antisemitism, "eliminationist antisemitism," as opposed to the garden variety characterized by defamation and discrimination, was uniquely German. Germans, Goldhagen contended, had an almost genetic predisposition towards killing Jews.

"Utter Nonsense!" exclaimed Mr. Müller.

In its place, Christopher Browning offered a "multicausal explanation of motivation." Most men, Browning found, became killers and a small minority (10%) did not, and suggested a half dozen intersecting explanations: "wartime brutalization, racism, segmentation and routinization of the task, special selection of the perpetrators, careerism, obedience to orders, deference to authority, ideological indoctrination, and conformity." Ordinary Germans did not have to be "of one mind," with Hitler's demonological views of the Jews to carry out genocide, he wrote. A combination of situational factors and ideological overlap was sufficient to turn "ordinary men" into Goldhagen's "willing executioners." Quoting from his book, I read the crucial passage summarizing the nub of Browning's argument and conclusion. "I noted," Browning wrote,

> the importance of conformity, peer pressure, and deference to authority, and . . . the legitimizing capacities of government. I also

---

13. See also *Sophie Scholl: The Final Days,* a film directed by Marc Rothemund.

emphasized the mutually intensifying effects of war and racism, as the years of anti-Semitic propaganda…dovetailed with the polarizing effects of war. I argued that nothing helped the Nazis to wage race war so much as the war itself, as the dichotomy of racially superior Germans and racially inferior Jews, central to Nazi ideology, could easily merge with the image of a beleaguered Germany surrounded by enemies, and concluded that if a group if normal middle-aged men could become killers under such circumstances, what group of men cannot?

"Human responsibility," Browning emphasized, "is ultimately an individual matter."

Unsurprisingly, everyone agreed that Goldhagen missed the mark completely. Cruelty, singled out by Montaigne as "the extreme of all vices," is not confined to a particular people, nation, religion, or what have you, the panel agreed. Interviews conducted at the Nuremberg War Crimes trials by the American psychiatrist Gustave Gilbert concluded that apart from out-and-out sadists, a small minority, the Nazi leadership showed no significant deviation from the norm. No less an authority as Anne Frank agreed: "There's in people," the diarist wrote on May 3, 1944, "simply an urge to destroy, to kill, to murder and rage, and until all mankind, without exception, undergoes a great change, war will be waged, everything that has been built up, cultivated, and grown will be destroyed and disfigured, after which mankind will have to begin all over again."

Franz Müller died in 2015, aged 90. The Scholls, he said, "were a sign that resistance was possible." Referring to *Kristallnacht*, the pogrom of November 1938, he mused: "we should have been out there demonstrating instead of taking cover in our homes while the terror was unfolding. To change the world," he added, as we polished off another bottle of Chateau Ste. Michelle, "is to start with oneself."

* * *

Chapter IV
Calmeyer's Riddle

One cannot tell the truth, I say, no book, I cannot, no one will ever be able to tell the truth, and that's too bad. And it's fortunate. Instead of that Illusion one can say everything and it will be invented truth. — Hélène Cixous[1]

1. "Righteous Among the Nations"

Jede Nacht war ich verzweifelt. Ich kam mir vor wie ein Mörder – I despaired every night. I saw myself as a murderer.
— Hans Georg Calmeyer in conversation with Dutch historian Ben Sijes, Osnabrück, July 12, 1967

Yad Vashem, the State of Israel's World Holocaust Remembrance Center, bestows the honorific "Righteous Among the Nations" on non-Jews who risked their lives to save Jews during the Holocaust. The medal struck by Israel's Holocaust authority to honor these "exemplars of great humanity" bears the Talmudic maxim "Whosoever saves a single life, saves an entire universe." Their names are enshrined in Yad Vashem's Avenue of the "Righteous Among the Nations." In 1992, Israel posthumously recognized Hans Georg Calmeyer as "Righteous Among the Nations." Yad Vashem estimated that the former

---

1. *Osnabrück Station to Jerusalem: A Memoir*, translated by Peggy Kamuf, Foreword by Eva Hoffman (New York: Fordham University Press, 2020), 57.

Rassereferent (Race Consultant) in occupied Netherlands had saved "at least 3,000 Jewish lives."

Calmeyer was born in Osnabrück in 1902 and died there in 1972. Abandoning his law practice, he entered the Netherlands with the invading forces in May of 1940. The following year saw him installed as Race Consultant at German headquarters in The Hague. Calmeyer's appointment was in the Department of Justice and Interior Affairs of the Reich Commissariat for the Occupied Dutch Territories. Headed by Friedrich Wimmer, the department covered legislation, internal administration justice (excluding police matters), culture, education, church affairs, public health, and youth. Calmeyer's duties comprised "Jewish Affairs," which boiled down to settling petitions in which Jews claimed to have been erroneously classified as Jews.

In January 1941, Jews in the Netherlands of "whole or partial Jewish blood" were required to register with the authorities. Race Consultant Calmeyer reviewed the appeals of Jews who disputed their "racial" classification. With the onset of the deportations in July 1942, Calmeyer's office was swamped with thousands of petitions from Jews who claimed to be Christians, sustaining the claims of roughly two out of every three.

Yad Vashem's imprimatur boosted local initiatives to name a dedicated peace center, a "peace lab," after the acclaimed *Judenretter* – "Osnabrück's Schindler." The building they had in mind was Villa Schlikker, former headquarters of the city's Nazi Party, aka *Das Braun Haus*. There, rounding out Osnabrück's Museum Quarter, it would join the Felix Nussbaum Haus and the Erich Remarque Peace Center,[2] honoring two other local and global celebrities. In other words, Osnabrück was going all out to live up to its self-image as *Friedensstadt*, City of Peace, a progressive and with-it place for living and visiting. In 1648, it had hosted the Peace of Westphalia terminating the Thirty Years War.

As for Calmeyer, the initiators had in mind a multi-media production with national appeal targeting fourteen-and-up-youths, a

---

2. Felix Nussbaum: Osnabrück 1904 – Auschwitz 1944; Erich Maria Remarque: Osnabrück 1898 – Switzerland 1970.

dynamic venue for raising historical and political awareness centered on Hans Calmeyer as a positive role model, a "drawing card" with the potential of attracting tens of thousands of visitors annually. While the unspeakable horrors of the Holocaust would get their due, the spotlight would be on the face of resistance, past and present. The project was to be financed from private and public funds. The museum, provisionally called the Hans Calmeyer Haus, was not expected to open its doors until 2020–21. That's where things stood at the end of 2017 and early 2018.

2. Femma's Riddle

On Monday May 4, 2020, Dutch television aired "Het raadsel van Femma" (Femma's Riddle). The hour-long documentary told the story of ninety-two-year-old Auschwitz survivor Femma Fleijsman. Mistakenly registered as the daughter of her mother's Jewish ex-husband, her real father, she said, was a non-Jewish window washer named Albertus Reijgwart. According to the documentary, Calmeyer dismissed the window-washer's desperate appeals and supporting documentation and threatened to classify Reijgwart, a Catholic from birth, as a Jew. Femma wound up in Auschwitz, aged 16.

The documentary lit a fuse under a long-simmering controversy. Articles in major newspapers, especially in the Netherlands, Germany, and Israel, ran with Femma's "riddle." That same month, an open letter signed by 275 scientists, artists, politicians, rabbis, and Holocaust survivors in the Netherlands and abroad, including Germany, urged

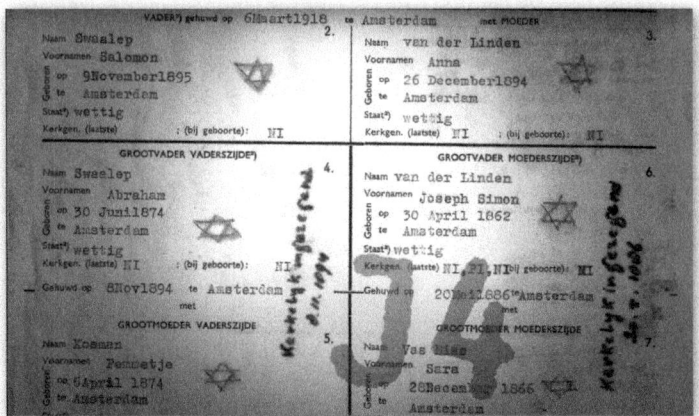

then chancellor Angela Merkel to deny funding for the project. "The undersigned," it stated, "wholeheartedly welcome the establishment of such a peace laboratory. Nevertheless, to name the building for Mr. Calmeyer is, in our opinion, inappropriate…. and runs counter to the very purpose it is meant to achieve."

> A museum that bears the name of Hans Calmeyer funded by the Federal Republic would, in our opinion, send the wrong message because it would serve to depreciate the destruction of the Jews. The option to appeal was consciously built into the system, serving to undermine resistance by covering up the systematic nature of the deportations. In addition, it served as a prophylactic mechanism designed to prevent "Aryans" from accidentally being affected by the anti-Jewish measures.

While acknowledging that the question of whether the race consultant was a rescuer or perpetrator admitted of no easy answer, what really mattered, the signatories underscored, was "that Calmeyer voluntarily joined the occupying authorities and actively participated in the destruction of at least 104,000 Jews…. If for no other reason, we can hardly call him a hero without reservation. He operated inside the system and acted within the parameters of the system, rarely deviating from the recommendations of his colleagues." They further noted that Yad Vashem was in the process of revisiting their decision. "We consider this re-examination appropriate and support it." A decision is expected in 2024.

3. Race Consultant

"On Wednesday, July 12, 1967, I visited attorney and notary H.G. Calmeyer in his office at Möserstrasse 10, in Osnabrück. We talked for more than 3.5 hours. We started at exactly nine o'clock."

"I" is Ben A. Sijes, a historian on the staff of the Netherlands Institute for War Documentation.[3] In 1967, the institute's director, Loe de Jong, was about to put the finishing touches on the first volume of *Het koninkrijk der Nederlanden in de tweede wereldoorlog* (The kingdom of the Netherlands in the Second World War), the standard narrative of the country's wartime ordeal. That first volume came out in 1969, the twenty-sixth, and final, in 1991. It was largely due to De Jong's research, based in turn on Calmeyer's say-so while in captivity in the Netherlands, that the onetime Race Consultant with the power over life and death metamorphosed into a Righteous Gentile. De Jong had never met the reputed rescuer of Jews and presumably dispatched his colleague to gather some last-minute impressions and specifics. Ben Sijes' first impression was that of a 'charmer,' a well-groomed, dapper, debonair, animated gent, with light gray hair, about the same height as himself, 1.7m [5.6 ft].

Some 25 years earlier, Calmeyer no doubt cut a fine figure in his uniform. Perhaps that's why, in 1939, Calmeyer donned the Wehrmacht uniform and joined the Wehrmacht. In *The Sleepwalkers*, Hermann Broch gave the "cult of the uniform" some serious thought, concluding that whoever "has worn a uniform for many years finds it a better organization of life than the man who merely exchanges one civilian suit in the evening for another civilian suit during the day." And not just any old uniform but one emblazoned with the swastika – in the eyes of the rescued, the perfect cover for subverting the "Final Solution" in the Netherlands.

---

3. Today's Netherlands Institute for War, Holocaust and Genocide Studies.

Two of Calmeyer's elder brothers had died in uniform in World War I. Was it to honor their memory that he coveted a uniform, or something rather more mundane, say a midlife crisis? A break with humdrum domesticity? He was thirty-six years old, married, a father, and practicing law. To his credit, Calmeyer never claimed to have joined the army and invade the Netherlands to save Jews.

4. Disenfranchisement, Expulsion, Annihilation

Much has been made of the fact that as a criminal defense lawyer Calmeyer had been disbarred (briefly, as it turned out) for having defended communists and, after 1933, had retained a Jewish secretary, Fräulein Hirsch, on account of her "outstanding performance," "impeccable work habits," and the likelihood of becoming unemployed.[4] Fräulein Hirsch lost her job, and it is safe to assume that she didn't get it back after Calmeyer's reinstatement.

---

4. Mathias Middelberg, "Calmeyer war ein Menschenretter" (Calmeyer was a rescuer), *Osnabrücker Geschichtsblog*, June 9, 2020. https://hvos.hypotheses

I looked for Fräulein Hirsch in the "Namen und Schicksale" (Names and Fates) registry of *Stationen auf dem Weg nach Auschwitz: Entrechtung, Vertreibung, Vernichtung, Juden in Osnabrück 1900–1945. Ein Gedenkbuch,* Peter Junk's and Martina Sellmeyer's unsurpassed study of the fate of Osnabrück's Jewish community.[5] The only likely candidate is Grete Hirsch, b. 1891; Grete Hirsch, however, was married. In 1933, Fräulein Hirsch was one of Osnabrück's 425 Jews; by war's end there were none.

In an article published on Osnabrück's History Blog in the fall of 2021, Martina Sellmeyer questioned Calmeyer's veracity as well as the company he kept.[6] In March 1947, Hans Georg Calmeyer declared that he had been "excluded from the legal profession on the grounds that I had demonstrated "communist sympathies." Nothing in Calmeyer's past, Sellmeyer notes, evinced a taste for the left. On the contrary, "the passionate collector of tin soldiers" had always been close to the right. As a student he joined a dueling fraternity; a year later he was enrolled in the Black Reichswehr, an extra-legal, right-wing paramilitary organization out to topple the Weimar Republic whose Munich branch was led by Ernst Roehm, the future chief of Hitler's Sturmabteilung (SA). Calmeyer studied with Karl Haushofer, whose geopolitical views on expansion – *Lebensraum* – left their mark on Hitler (the fact that Haushofer was married to a Jew the Führer took into the bargain). Next, Calmeyer joined the National Socialist Motor Brigade (NSKK) and the National Socialist Association of Legal Professionals (NSRB). In Munich, he roomed with fellow student and Osnabrück native

---

.org/5194 (accessed January 10, 2023). Middelberg is the author of the Calmeyer biography *Wer bin ich, dass ich über Leben und Todt entscheide? Hans Calmeyer – "Rassereferent" in der Niederlanden 1941–1945* (Göttingen: Wallstein Verlag, 2015). (Who am I to decide about life and death? – Hans Calmeyer – "Race Consultant" in the Netherlands 1941–1945).

5. Junk and Junk Sellmeyer, *Stationen,* 283. See Chapter 1, fn. 8.

6. Martina Sellmeyer, "Der 'Judenretter' verteidigt den Osnabrücker Kreisleiter – Calmeyers fragwürdige Allianzen" (The 'rescuer of Jews' defends Osnabrück's District Leader Osnabrücker – Calmeyer's questionable alliances), *Osnabrücker Geschichtsblog,* September 11, 2021(https://hvos.hypotheses.org /6028 (accessed January 23, 2023).

Eberhard Westerkamp, a zealous advocate of *völkisch* ideas, attended a Nazi Party event showcasing Hitler, and took part in Hitler's attempted Beer Hall Putsch, not as a Hitler follower but as a member of the Black Reichswehr. In 1946, Calmeyer declared that this experience marked the end of his flirtation with National Socialism.

Calmeyer's flagging interest in National Socialism seems not to have dampened his friendship with Munich roommate Eberhard Westerkamp (1903–1980). Westerkamp joined the SA in 1933 and held an administrative post in Osnabrück until 1940, the year he set out for Poland and served under Governor-General Hans Frank, aka the "Butcher of Poland." In Poland, recounts Sellmeyer, Westerkamp spoke out in favor of rounding Jews up in ghettos and signed off on a proposal to impose the death penalty on escapees. Yet the Governor-General's no-holds-barred approach to the "the Jewish Question" seemingly triggered a *crise de conscience*, prompting Westerkamp's resignation in January 1942. Selmeyer notes that, in contrast, the Race Consultant chose to remain at this post.

Westerkamp later fought on the Russian front, and after the war testified against the High Command of the Wehrmacht and at the Nuremberg War Crimes trials. From there he went on to serve Lower Saxony as State Secretary in the Ministry of the Interior and President of the German Red Cross. "He and Calmeyer remained lifelong friends."

Westermark was not the only committed National Socialist in Calmeyer's entourage. Oskar Laue, a manufacturer with close ties to the SS, helped secure the dismissed lawyer's reinstatement, and so did Osnabrück NSDAP Kreisleiter (Nazi Party District Leader) Wilhelm Münzer, Calmeyer's future colleague in the Reich Commissariat for the Occupied Dutch Territories, and Dr. Carlo Stüler, his boss in The Hague and affable dinner host.[7]

---

7. Martin Sijes, "Hans Calmeyer: Ein Gerechter unter den Völkern?" (Hans Calmeyer: A Righteous Among the Nations?), *Osnabrückner Geschichtsblog*, November 21, 2021. https://hvos.hypotheses.org/6180 (accessed February 27, 2023).

Panikos Panayi's detailed study of the Jews of Osnabrück, "before, during and after the Third Reich," determined that "small numbers of people" were responsible for orchestrating the anti-Jewish campaign there and that most people simply stood by.[8] Even so, on August 20, 1935, roughly thirty percent of Osnabrück's population, "twenty-five to thirty thousand comrades," took part in "A Mass Rally on the Jewish Question."[9]

"It's here, beneath the windows of the Jonas House, that Omi used to watch the streets and the squares fill up to overflowing with a crowd drunk on hatred, and banners of the Reich, which gave it the brilliance of a terrible opera, came up to her balcony."[10]

---

8. Panikos Panayi, "Victims, Perpetrators and Bystanders in a German Town: The Jews of Osnabrück Before, During and After the Third Reich," *European History Quarterly*, Volume 33(4), 480–81, 485.

9. Ibid., 467.

10. Cixous, *Osnabrück*, preface, xxiv. "Omi" was Cixous' grandmother. She joined daughter Ève in Oran, Algeria, shortly after *Kristallnacht*. In Osnabrück, "Omi" lived with her brother Andreas Jonas. Photo in Hélène Cixous, *Well-Kept Ruins*, trans. Beverley Bie Brahic (London, New York, Calcutta: Seagull

Kreisleiter Wilhem Münzer, a fanatical Nazi, drove the "Aryaniza-tion" process in Osnabrück. "[T]he expropriation of the largest Jewish businesses," he informed an enthusiastic crowd, was "slowly moving forward and without friction.… This brings joy and stirs up the blood. (Loud applause)."[11]

Münzer's Jew-baiting comrade-in-arms was watchmaker Erwin Kolkmeyer. At Christmas "he made posters proclaiming *Christliche Weihnacht = Judischer Verdienst* ("Christian Christmas, Jewish Profit"). Jews were closing in. Soon Germans would no longer be able to live in Osnabrück. Half a century after Jews had been granted legal residency, *lebt der schaffende Deutsche Mensch demnach in Hinternhausern und Kellerwohnungen*… "hard-working Germans are being driven into basements and backyard sheds.…"[12] "[T]he very face of terror,"[13] Kolkmeyer was the chief culprit in the torching of Osnabrück's syna-gogue in "the night of broken glass," November 9, 1938.

Osnabrück's Jews are gone, as has Wertheim's Deutsche Herren-mode, the Jewish-owned men's fashions store "two steps away from Kolkmeyer's watchmaker and jewelry shop"… but "the Kolkmeyer shop window has gotten much bigger. "[14]

In trials held in 1949 assessing accountability "for the destruc-tion and plundering of the synagogue, Jewish businesses, and the deportation of the Jewish men to the Buchenwald concentration camp," Kolkmeyer "received a sentence of just ten months because much of the evidence against him was rejected." As for Münzer, "character witnesses described him as a deeply religious person who wouldn't hurt a soul." Without exception the accused, including the chief of police, denied having taken part in the *Reichskristallnacht*. Münzer feigned complete ignorance and testified not to have learned

---

Books, 2022), 4. The caption reads: "This photograph of the famous Jonas house at 2 Nikolaiort, Osnabrück, was taken by Lichtenberg, the renowned early-twentieth-century photographer."

11. Sellmeyer and Junk, *Stationen*, 140.
12. Cisoux, *Osnabrück* 105. Jews had not been allowed in Osnabrück until 1880.
13. Ibid., 34.
14. Ibid., 117.

about the synagogue's incineration until the morning after. From his housekeeper. And, unlike Kreisleiters elsewhere, claimed not to have received the order, nor of having passed it on.[15]

Calmeyer successfully defended Münzer in the postwar denazification process. "Why," Sellmeyer asks, "did Calmeyer represent a fanatical and incorrigible National Socialist? What bound the two?... How much contact was there between them during their service in the Reich Commissariat in the Netherlands? Did Münzer have something on Calmeyer that could have caused him problems after 1945?"

Sellmeyer concluded "Der 'Judenretter'" with a quotation from Paulo Coehlo: *Judge me by the people I avoid.*

5. Calmeyer's Modus Operandi

Dutch historian Loe de Jong's history of the Second World War in the Netherlands surveyed the muddle occasioned by the enactment of the "most fateful decree in the years of occupation": Decree VO 6/41 required the registration of all Jews residing in the Netherlands. The January 1941 decree defined "Jew" in the broadest possible terms: all it took was one Jewish grandparent. Article 4/3: "A grandparent is deemed a full Jew, if he or she was at any time a member of a Jewish religious congregation." A non-Jewish grandparent who had belonged to the Jewish religious congregation, or still belonged to it (in some mixed marriages it sometimes happened that the non-Jewish partner had become Jewish); if so, then that grandparent was considered Jewish, and thus the grandchild as well. Doubtful cases were sent to Calmeyer's office.

Among the 140,000 so-called Volljuden ("full Jews") – all persons whose grandparents included three or more full Jews by race – there were thousands who didn't qualify for deportation, at least not under the rules that prevailed in the opening phase. "By June 1941," writes the Dutch historian, Calmeyer "had already received more than a thousand such doubtful cases," many of which, the Race Consultant

---

15. Junk and Sellmeyer, *Stationen*, 259.

found, had registered unnecessarily. Calmeyer, De Jong emphasized, "was neither a member of the Nazi Party nor a racial fanatic, and as a rule was inclined to consider the doubt well founded." A woman, for example, might claim that the child registered as Jewish was in fact the issue of an extramarital affair with a Christian, and thus not Jewish. Calmeyer agreed, but required proof: old letters, declarations from persons with access to the facts, as well as a "formal declaration" in the presence of an official of the civil registry. Many such declarations, noted De Jong, were made in good faith, though not all. "I approached my job, and certainly initially," Calmeyer asserted after the war, "strictly by the book, giving little thought that deception might be involved." Accordingly, he proceeded with utmost caution and rejected some applications that should have been considered valid. De Jong estimates that before the start of the deportations in July of 1942, Calmeyer favorably decided roughly 1,000 cases. The second phase was far more important, given that lives were at stake. But even in the first stage, the Race Consultant's modus operandi had not gone undetected and raised eyebrows among the henchmen of the "Final Solution" in the Netherlands. But at no time was he suspected of fraud.

With race the crucial factor, it made no sense, Calmeyer argued, to base Jewishness solely on belonging to a religious congregation; membership in a Jewish religious congregation wasn't necessarily synonymous with being a Jew; a non-Jewish woman might have joined because of her husband. Department head Friedrich Wimmer, remarked De Jong, "lackadaisical as always, postponed the decision," by and large leaving it up to his subordinate to decide.[16]

In Germany, a husband and wife in a mixed marriage were not deported, on the grounds that deporting one but not the other was bound to cause trouble. Calmeyer argued for the same arrangement – known as Privileged Mixed Marriages – in the Netherlands. Growing up in Amsterdam, I personally knew of one such case. My brother and I called her *Oma* ("grandma"). Oma was not Jewish but married to one. The couple had two daughters. The older one, Chellie, was married

16. L. de Jong, *Het Koninkrijk der Nederlanden in the Tweede Wereldoorlog*, Vol. 5, March '41–July '42, Part 1 (S-'Gravenhage: Staatsuitgeverij, 1974), 508–511; Vol. 6, Part 1, 1975, 50–54.

to a Jew. Oma claimed that Chellie was the issue of an extramarital affair with a non-Jew. A Christian man had come forward prepared to vouch for it. Chellie's husband, Aaron, was interned in Westerbork, where his mixed marriage status kept him from deportation to the East. Chellie's younger sister wound up in Ravensbrück, the women's concentration camp in Germany (she survived). I can't say whether Calmeyer had a hand in this. Verily, separating the Christian "wheat"' from the Jewish "chaff" was no sinecure.

6. Window Washers of the World Unite

The Calmeyer option seems not to have had much traction in the lower echelons of the working class. Both the documentary and the eponymous book on which it is based, Els van Diggele's *Het raadsel van Femma: Prooi van een mensenredder* (Femma's riddle: a rescuer's prey), exposed the class character of Calmeyer's decision. "That sounds like a reasonable interpretation," acknowledged the documentary's maker Alfred Edelstein. "But if true," added the director of the Jewish programming division of the Holland's Evangelical Broadcaster, "it requires a closer look at the people Calmeyer chose to sacrifice." As for the Jews he rescued, Edelstein elaborated,

> they tended to be the well-to-do, educated, cultured. Many were German Jews who fled to the Netherlands. What we hadn't heard, at least not until Femma stepped forward, are the testimonies of ordinary Jewish people, vendors, bakers, carpenters, ragpick-ers, the daughters of window washers. Almost none of these sur-vived to testify. Maybe they weren't considered important enough to save. Our goal was not to underwrite the Fleijsman family's judgment, nor to distance ourselves from it, but to shed light on Calmeyer's conduct... canonized in De Jong's opus, culled from the perspective of the saved.... The 'riddle' is meant to give the children of window washers a voice.... From the victims' perspec-tive, Calmeyer doesn't appear quite so virtuous.[17]

---

17. "Femmas lijdensweg sinds 1943 zaait anno 2020 paniek" (Femma's or-deal since 1943 sews panic), October 1, 2020, https://www.ewmagazine

Van Diggele dedicated her book "To the children of window washers who didn't come back."[18]

"So it should not come as a surprise," observed Johannes Max van Ophuijsen, a signatory to the letter requesting Chancellor Merkel deny funding for the Calmeyer project,

> That her sons, now in advanced middle age, but formed and deformed by the compulsive mechanisms that enabled their mother to cope with her repressed memories back in the 'fifties, are to this day willing to carry sandwich boards through the streets of Osnabrück proclaiming *Keine Ehre für Calmeyer!* [No Honor for Calmeyer!] No matter how preposterous and absurd both the evil rules and regulations and the compromised anomalies and grounds for this or any other exception may have been, it takes a particularly unashamed elitist hardness of heart to miss the point of Van Diggele's dedication of her book.[19]

Virtually the entire Dutch Jewish proletariat was wiped out during the occupation. Lacking the wherewithal and connections to go into hiding, poor and working-class Jews were at the mercy of the occupier.

At the end of the documentary, which was also broadcast in Israel, a spokeswoman for Yad Vashem said that it would reexamine Calmeyer's "Righteous Gentile" award. A crucial factor for such a reversal "may be," in the award's definition, "that the same rescuer was involved in murder, war crimes, or harm to others," a clause inserted after Calmayer's installation on the Avenue of the Righteous in 1992.

.nl/opinie/achtergrond/2020/10/femmas-lijdensweg-sinds-1943-zaait-anno
-2020-paniek-779735/?utm_referrer=https%3A%2F%2Fduckduckgo.com%2F
(accessed January 17, 2023). Cf. Hélène Cixous: "For children-who-survived of parents who barely survived, says my daughter, an unbearable pain and a source of guilt, says my daughter." *Osnabrück*, 120.
18. "Didn't come back" was how survivors and families of survivors were wont to refer to the murdered. "So-and-so didn't come back," rather than "So-and-so was murdered, killed."
19. Johannes Max van Ophuijsen, "'Indifferent Honest'? The Posthumous Charm of a Rassenreferent," *Osnabrücker Geschichtsblog*, September 27, 2022. http://hvos.hypotheses.org/7987 (accessed March 1, 2023).

The phrase "not to commit murder, war crimes, or harm" carries special weight "in instances where potential 'Righteous Among the Nations' have, on the one hand, directly or indirectly prevented murder, war crimes or harm through their actions, but on the other hand are responsible for acts that have (in)directly led to murder, war crimes or harm." Calmeyer supporters attach more weight to the number of people who were not deported, the larger number, than to the smaller number of Jews who had their applications rejected and deported.

"The world wants to be lied to and would rather hear from a rescuer than about someone who sent people to their death," Van Dingele wrote in her book. "Calmeyer operated within the system and was part of it from almost the beginning until the very end...The unit Calmeyer headed in 1943 registered some 500 people as Jews whom it determined were mistakenly considered Aryan, according to Van Diggele. Those people never approached Calmeyer's office...Femma Fleijsman was among some 1,000 applicants with legitimate appeals Calmeyer that arbitrarily rejected."[20]

Van Diggele's opposite number is historian Petra Van den Boomgaard. Van den Boomgaard earned a doctorate with a dissertation on the former Race Consultant: *Calmeyer: Voor de nazi's geen Jood* (2019) (Calmeyer: not a Jew to the Nazis). When Calmeyer reviewed Fleijsman's case, she told the Jewish Telegraph Agency, it was also being audited by two Dutch Nazis. This made it vastly more difficult for Calmeyer to go easy on Fleijsman. Van Diggele, asserted Van den Boogaard, "is angry and basically using Femma's wartime story at the expense of a facts-based narrative."[21]

20. Canaan Lipshiz, "Did Hans Calmeyer Send a Jewish Woman to Auschwitz?" *The Jerusalem Post,* May 7, 2020. https://www.jpost.com/diaspora/antisemitism/did-hans-calmeyer-send-a-jewish-woman-to-auschwitz-627181 (accessed January 17, 2023).
21. Ibid.

7. Debate Without End

In the year 2000, the "City of Peace" engaged Dutch historian Geraldien von Frijtag Drabbe Künzel to prepare an unbiased opinion *in re* Calmeyer. The upshot of the historian's investigation was that Calmeyer had indeed signed off on specious claims, but that no corresponding intent could be deduced from this.

Subsequently, the Netherlands Institute for War Documentation and Genocide Studies commissioned von Frijtag Drabbe Künzel to expand her findings. *Het geval Calmeyer* (The Calmeyer case), Künzel's "contextual biography," came out in 2008. Although the book covers Calmeyer's entire life, the main focus is on 1941–45. Discarding the "good" v. "bad" construct, Künzel strove to situate Calmeyer in his historical context, from the vantage point of his time. A Künzel-vetted summary by Osnabrück archivist Thomas Brakmann surfaced on the city's History Blog on June 6, 2020.[22]

To Künzel, writes Brakmann, Calmeyer was not a perpetrator in the sense that he himself killed Jews, but "he was on the side of the perpetrators," not someone who observed the tragedy from the sidelines. Calmeyer actively sought employment with the occupation regime…in Holland and owed his appointment to nepotism. Strong National Socialist convictions was not a prerequisite for the job, nor administrative experience. To be posted in occupied Netherlands – "a new world in which to make a new beginning" (Calmeyer) – was a "relatively safe" career move, a refuge. In a letter to his wife, he referred to it as a "new world, "his colony."

> In the four years Calmeyer worked in the occupier's administration he was deeply involved in the exclusion and discrimination of Jews. He did not protest publicly, not even when thousands of Jews were taken from their homes and transported like cattle. He witnessed at least one roundup, registering their impotence and fear of death. His decisions could spell the difference between staying or leaving

---

22. "Der Fall Calmeyer ('Het geval Calmeyer') – eine Zusammenfassung" (The Calmeyer case – a summary) https://hvos.hypotheses.org/5180 (accessed January 20, 2023).

for an unknown destination. He stated after the war that he knew they would be murdered, and, by rejecting hundreds of petitions, condemned hundreds to death.

Although initially Calmeyer couldn't have known what he was getting into, Brakmann proceeded, "the fact that he referred to 'resettlement' as early as the spring of 1941 suggests that he had an idea of what lay ahead." In the first phase, centered for the most part on the Jews' administrative exclusion, Germany's Race Consultant played a leading and coordinating role. With the occupier dependent on the Dutch authorities to implement the registration requirement, Calmeyer turned out to be a good fit. The very fact that he did not behave as a ferocious zealot or a rabid Jew-hater, but as a "politically independent, well-mannered, cultured lawyer, made him acceptable to his Dutch counterparts in the Ministry of the Interior, overwhelmingly stocked with civil servants in the Dutch administrative tradition of adaptation and subordination."

After the war, the Dutch detained Calmeyer on suspicion of war crimes. In the 1960s, however, with renewed interest in the Holocaust in the Netherlands and Europe, the onetime Race Consultant was no longer suspected of war crimes but emerged as a resister and a witness rather than defendant.

"This transition," observed Brakmann,

> influenced the way Calmeyer judged his own conduct and that of others. The statements he made in the forties are mostly defensive, deploying arguments resembling those by Dutch high officials who remained in office. They said that they had remained in their posts 'to prevent worse.' By 'worse' they meant various things: replacement by members of the Dutch National Socialist Party, chaos in the administration; Germans taking complete, extreme control. In Calmeyer's case, the 'worse' thing to be avoided was, number one, allowing matters of descent to fall into the hands of the Security Police and, two, the reversal of decisions arrived at.

Calmeyer, Brakmann noted as well, was intelligent enough to realize that he was a cog in the system and shunned taking risks that could have jeopardized his job. Perhaps he wanted to keep his position in the interest of helping this or that individual, as he claimed after the war. But this rescue effort was offset by his cooperation in the unmitigated discrimination, robbery, exclusion, and expulsion of the Jews. "He felt guilty about this, possibly even then, but certainly afterwards.... The depression and fatigue that bothered him in his twilight years were undoubtedly related to this split self-image."

In the end, Künzel's findings sustained the principal argument broached in the open letter addressed to Germany's chancellor: that Calmeyer "voluntarily joined the occupying authorities and actively participated in the destruction of at least 104,000 Jews."

Arguably, Calmeyer's staunchest champion is his biographer Matthias Middelberg.[23] Osnabrück-born attorney and politician (Christian Democratic Union), Middelberg published an 18-page article, "Calmeyer Was a Rescuer" on June 9, 2020, three days after Brakmann's article and undoubtedly a response to it.

Middelberg submitted a point-by-point rebuttal to Calmeyer's critics. He claimed that Van Diggele's book lacked substance; that Calmeyer was not a Nazi, an antisemite, nor a "stinknormaler Opportunist" ("ordinary opportunist"); that he didn't persecute Jews but saved many by removing their names from the deportation lists. He conceded that he was part of the system but didn't function like a cog, but often took positions that deviated from the norm, admitting evidence of non-Jewish that was unacceptable back home.

Nor, according to Middelberg, did Calmeyer "contribute to the deportations simply by virtue of his role in deciding the applications," as alleged by the signatories to the letter addressed to Chancellor Merkel. Moreover, the biographer contended, processing Femma's application gave her a year's reprieve from deportation (October 1942–43). Deferment afforded an opportunity to look for alternate ways to avoid deportation, by going into hiding, say. Furthermore, Calmeyer argued that, in contradistinction to the *Ostjuden* (Eastern European Jews), Holland's Portuguese Jews were not "racially" Jewish, and thus should be allowed to emigrate to Portugal. Not surprisingly,

---

23. See fn. 4.

the proposal fell on deaf ears. Calmeyer employed "the idiom of the racial fanatic," the better to sabotage the system, and deviated from the norm in allowing lawyers to be part of the process. Not that the SS was asleep. By the fall of 1943, Middelberg conceded, Calmeyer boosted the number of negative decisions, including Femma's. In March 1944, Eichmann's representatives in the Netherlands started inspecting his files, but there never would be a full-scale investigation, not with the Allied invasion on the horizon.

Middelberg compared Calmeyer to a doctor with 50 life-saving pills for 5,000 deathly ill people and an officer on the *Titanic* deciding whom to save and whom to let drown.[24] "He [Calmeyer] took on 40 drowning passengers. Twenty others swam towards the boat. He knows that if he takes on any more the boat will capsize. He pulls away. Does he save 40 or does he take the blame for the 20 who died?"

"Protesting the anti-Jewish measures, as some have suggested, would have landed Calmeyer in a concentration camp" [*sic*]. Without Calmeyer, and without his sabotage, at least 3,000 more individuals would have become Holocaust victims." "There are," the CDU deputy acknowledged, "survivors, or family of the murdered, whose petitions the lawyer rejected, and merely think of him as part of the murder machine. Femma Fleijesman-Swaalep was one of these."

For Middelberg, the ultimate proof was in the Israeli pudding: "Yad Vashem was aware of his ambivalent roll and yet declared him 'Righteous.'"

8. Triage

Middelberg's "amicus brief" conceded that in addition to subjective interpretations "there may also be an objective one, at least one that takes a stab at an overarching view. All perspectives," he asserted, "must be considered in the design and the naming of the planned museum in Osnabrück's Villa Schlikker."

---

24. The *Titanic* had 2,200 passengers, divided into three separate classes. There were twenty lifeboats for 1,178 people, with many putting to sea only half-filled.

CAMILLA "SARA" SPIRA

Aanmeldingsformulier voor één persoon, die geheel of gedeeltelijk van joodschen bloede is (Verordening 6/1941)

Middelberg's defense included the application form "for one person of full or part Jewish blood (VO 6/1941)." Spira, "Sara" Camilla, born in Hamburg in 1906; last German address, Berlin. Married to Dr. Herman "Israel" Eisner, Jewish. Last residence, Amsterdam. Two Jewish grandparents. Applied March 14, 1941. Signed. "8" established that on May 9, 1940 (the day before the German invasion) she belonged to the Jewish community and married to a Jew. "9" states that she has two Jewish grandparents. "Filled out truthfully," March 13, 1941.

Camilla Spira was a German film and stage actor. In Westerbork she took part in the camp's entertainment life. Calmeyer approved her application, releasing her from the transit camp. And thus, writes Middelberg, Camilla Spira was eventually declared fully Aryan. Her marriage to Hermann Eisner qualified as a "privileged mixed marriage," so that in addition to herself, her husband and children also avoided deportation. Camilla Spira survived the war. Her family card at Amsterdam's City Archive indicates that she moved back to Berlin in July 1947.

LAUREEN NUSSBAUM

Camilla Spira's case resembled that of Laureen Nussbaum. Born Hannelore Klein in 1927, Laureen was eight years old when her family quit Germany and settled in Amsterdam. Their new home, like that of many better-off German Jews who had flocked to Amsterdam after 1933, was in the city's Rivers Quarter.

In the late spring of 2019, Nussbaum, a retired professor of German Studies at Oregon's Portland State University, was invited to Osnabrück, where she addressed a group of young people. Hans Calmeyer, she said, was "a quiet hero" who saved "at least 3,700 Jews from deportation and death."[25]

> The short version: My mother was the illegitimate child of a singer from Austria – a Catholic – and her German-Jewish admirer. His mother, however, didn't want him to marry a non-Jewish woman. My grandmother left her daughter, Mia, in care of a Protestant family in Dresden and pursued her profession for another 14 years, before settling in Vienna in 1913, when she took Mia back in.... Mother and daughter always spent the summer holidays with the girl's father, Berthold. Mia's Jewish grandmother died in 1919, whereupon her parents finally married. At this time, Mia was officially recognized by Berthold as his daughter and from then on bore his surname.

25. Laureen Nussbaum. "Hans Calmeyer ist 'ein stiller Held'," June 16, 2020, https://hvos.hypotheses.org/5226 (accessed February 25, 2023).

In 1941, we were ordered to register with the authorities. My mother truthfully claimed that she had two Jewish grandparents. Since she was married to a Jew, we were considered a Jewish family. It soon became apparent that we were in a precarious situation. Mother's father had died in 1928. My mother and her non-Jewish mother, the former singer, now did everything they could to prove that Berthold had not been my mother's biological father, and in 1919 had only recognized her as his daughter, so that she would bear his name instead of her mother's maiden name.

Our Amsterdam lawyer, Nino Kotting, advised my mother to look for a plausible biological father. The Dresden foster father, who had signed her school reports for years, seemed the best choice. But his widow firmly rejected this encumbrance.... Besides, all foreign mail was subject to censorship! Thus, important documentation was missing in my mother's application for Aryanization, which had already been submitted to Calmeyer's office in May 1942, i.e., before the start of the systematic deportations of Jews from Holland.

On August 6, my mother, sisters, and I were arrested during a raid in our neighborhood, but released when it turned out that our name was on the "Calmeyer List."...

I now come to the extremely important relief strategy, which Dr. Middelberg rightly emphasizes in his book *Who am I that I decide about life and death?*, but does not mention in his article "Calmeyer Was a Rescuer." This is the reversal of the burden of proof. In his notes to my mother's application, Calmeyer writes that my mother was undeniably the illegitimate daughter of an Aryan mother and that therefore there was no reason to assume that her biological father was a Jew. His office was unable to produce evidence that my mother had been fathered by a Jew. My mother's request was thus approved and we – our mother, my sisters and I – and in January 1943 were able to remove the yellow star from our clothes. Hence the title of my book *Shedding Our Stars*.[26] My father, who

---

26. Laureen Nussbaum with Karen Kirtley, *Shedding Our Stars: The Story of*

was not on the "Calmeyer List," was sufficiently protected by his "privileged mixed marriage." People like him are certainly among those rescued by Calmeyer, but, as far as I know, are not officially recorded as such.

THE BLAASERS[27]

Maria Catharina Kreveld, was born in Belgium, January 9, 1909; Benjamin in 1903, in Amsterdam. Maria and Benjamin were married in 1929, also in Belgium. They settled in Amsterdam in 1930. Benjamin had a hard time making ends meet; the Social Welfare office considered him a "deadbeat." To be sure, Benjamin Blaaser was often in trouble, in and out of jail, including that time "he was found in a location off-limits to Jews." Maria Blaaser-Kreveld had her hands full keeping the family's many heads above water, relying for the most part on the dole as a first and last resort.[28]

The Blaasers divorced in the summer of 1942. On October 12, 1942, "around three in the afternoon," Benjamin Blaaser, prisoner 13290, was murdered in Camp Mauthausen, the stone-quarrying camp in Austria. Blaaser's camp papers included a Death Certificate. Its eighteen parts ranged from family data – name and address, religion ("Mosaic"), nationality, adult children (none), minors – to questions concerning his "estate": whether there were any assets in his name or funds: bonds, securities, investments, property, real and liquid, debts, etc., and, if so, what steps had been taken to secure these. As every category relating to possible assets had been left blank, the Mauthausen district court saw no point in taking the inquest any further.

To keep from being deported, Blaaser-Kreveld was doing her utmost to downplay the Jewish connection and foregrounding her Christian

Hans Calmeyer and How He Saved Thousands of Families Like Mine (Berkeley, California: She Writes Press, 2019). No relation to the painter Felix Nussbaum.

27. More on "the Blaasers," in English, including photographs, at https://www.joodsmonument.nl/en/page/177964/benjamin-blaaser.

28. Adapted from Guus Luijters, "Rapenburg 26-huis, Amsterdam," in *Joodse huizen 5: verhalen over vooroorlogse bewoners* (Jewish houses: stories about prewar residents) (https://gibbonuitgeefagentschap.nl/, 2019) 143–55.

heritage. An undated letter informed Welfare that she had "nothing against my children having to wear a star.[29] You should know, however,

> that my sons have not been circumcised, and thus not Jewish. I am a Christian. My five-year-old daughter attends a Christian school. My four-and-a-half-year-old son will be attending a Christian school after the summer holidays as well, hence my children don't belong in a Jewish school, even though they have three Jewish grandparents. [Starting October 1, 1941, Jewish children were to attend separate schools.] They are not registered with the Jewish community. I hope you will investigate this.

Even so, she wore the yellow star.

In April 1943, Social Welfare reported that the Kreveld flat was without water, incredibly dirty, and that the "J" was still on her identity card,[30] adding that "the extent to which she is Jewish, or Christian, is something the Reichskommissar has to determine" – i.e., Hans Calmeyer. Maria Kreveld seems to have had no problem establishing her Christian heritage. On July 12, Welfare reported, "she remained seven weeks with her children in the Jewish Theater and was released on September 7. Her identity card bears Calmeyer stamp No. 30278." Ten days later, the same agency noted that "she was one of eleven illegitimate children and in possession of Dr. Calmeyer-stamp 39276." The next entry, October 9, 1943, recorded that the family was sent to the Jewish Theater and suggested "writing off 15.50 guilders in debt."

Maria Catharina Kreveld appeared to have an open and shut case. This would seem to take legal representation out of the equation. On the other hand, an undated letter to the school mentioned an appointment with a lawyer and requested Harry be excused from attending. "This may have to do with her divorce, but another possibility is an appointment with one of Calmeyer's lawyers," speculates Guus Luijters, the chronicler of the Blaasers' fate. "Proof of non-Jewishness would spare her and her children from deportation."[31]

---

29. Introduced May 3, 1942, for individuals and residences.
30. Introduced January 23, 1942.
31. Guus Luijters, "Rapenburg 26," 152.

Kreveld's Jewish Council card recorded that she had been divorced and that she and her children entered Westerbork on October 28, 1943, and locked up in Barrack 67, the Punishment Barrack. Had she been caught outdoors without the Jewish star? Was it because she had not one but two Calmeyer stamps? The card also notes that Maria Catharina and seven of her eight children were transported in a cattle car that left Westerbork on January 25, 1944, and gassed in Auschwitz upon arrival.

The train that took the Blaasers to their death passed through Osnabrück, "the only city in Germany that has at its disposal railway-wise all the cardinal directions."[32] As a railroad junction, it was bombed repeatedly.

JANUARY 27

948 Jews from Westerbork arrive with an RSHA transport from Holland. In the transport are 391 men, 435 women, and 122 children. After the selection, 190 men, given Nos. 172860–173049, and 69 women, given Nos. 74902–74970, are admitted to the camp. The remaining 689 people are killed in the gas chambers.[33]

9. The End of the Affair?

Osnabrück's "Peace Lab" was conceived as "a place of teaching about racism and exclusion," an active forum for reflection. A prospectus issued in January 2023 outlined its educational mission, feasibility, cost, and schedule. However, it was no longer to be named after Calmeyer.

On Thursday, April 27, 2023, the *Osnabrücker Zeitung* reported the outcome of a meeting of the city council regarding the naming of the museum. "Täter oder Menschenretter?" – "Perpetrator or Rescuer"[34] – confirmed that the city had backed off from naming the museum after Calmeyer. Two names had been considered and

---

32. Cixous, *Osnabrück*, 86.
33. *Auschwitz Chronicle*, 577.
34. "Täter oder Menschenretter?" *Osnabrücker Zeitung*, Thursday, April 27,

voted upon: "Forum Calmeyer – Perpetrator or Rescuer?" and "The Villa – Forum Remembrance and Contemporary History," with the majority settling for the latter, a bland designation not likely to offend anyone. "Villa Schlikker" was rejected because of its association with the Nazi past.

The article further reported that Yad Vashem had not yet decided whether to strip Calmeyer of his 1992 "Righteous Gentile" award, despite the city's ongoing requests for clarity. Yad Vashem's decision to revisit the award had taken the wind out of the sails of the "Calmeyer Museum" advocates.

An inset explained that the former Osnabrück lawyer Race Consultant had saved 3,000 Jews from deportation by accepting falsified documents while sending hundreds of Jews to certain death so as not to draw attention to himself. "This dilemma troubled Calmeyer for the rest of his life and comprises the core of the future museum."

*   *   *

2023, page 9. I am indebted to Thomas Brakmann, head of the Osnabrück division of the Lower Saxony's State Archive, for alerting me to this article.

Postscript: Hélène Cixous, Erich Maria Remarque, Felix Nussbaum

HÉLÈNE CIXOUS

Osnabrück is rather proud of its celebrities. It doesn't boast of them. It thanks them, it's an honor, no one ever imagined the E.M. Remarque or Felix Nussbaum or my mother could remain in Osnabrück after having obtained the Abitur [successful completion of secondary education]. Osnabrück always expected these detachments. It's natural. It's a good nurse for little ones and then for the dead.[35]   – Hélène Cixous

Osnabrück does not offer condemned ones the slim chances of survival that vast, complicated Berlin grants. Here, the entire city is a simple mousetrap. The little mice people have no chance. Not one escapes. Neither the Nussbaum family. Nor the van Pels family. Nor the Remarque family. Nor the Jonas family. Nor.[36]

– Hélène Cixous

Unlike Hans Georg Calmeyer, Felix Nussbaum, and Erich Maria Remarque, Hélène Cixous was not from Osnabrück but Oran, Algeria. Osnabrück was the city of her mother, Ève Cisoux-Klein. Born in Strasburg in 1910, Ève Cixous-Klein grew up in Osnabrück, and settled in Algeria in 1929 (she was expelled in 1971 and settled in France). Ève's sister, Èrika, followed suit in 1933. Hélène's grandmother, Rosalie Klein – "Omi" – a war widow, was born in 1882, two years after Jews were legally permitted to reside in Osnabrück. "Omi" joined daughter Ève in Algeria in November 1938, shortly after *Kristallnacht*.

Ève Cisoux-Klein visited Osnabrück in 1985, as a guest of the municipality, a goodwill gesture towards its "former Jews." "[T]he people are very nice, they received us very well," she writes to Hélène

---

35. Cixous, *Osnabrück*, 116.
36. Ibid., xxv. The van Pels, Dutch citizens, hid with the Frank family in Amsterdam. In Anne's diary, they are the van Daans.

in Oran, "the hotel was nice, the streets clean, stately houses, nothing but department stores, the restaurant gemütlich and gut. Morgen ist ein busy day with the mayor, a woman."[37] Hélène: "[…] the city has become feminist, it has always been with the times."[38]

When Ève and Èrika visited Osnabrück in 1985, Hélène decided not to join them. It was their "thing." Hélène's knowledge about Osnabrück came from her mother and information gleaned from Peter Junk's and Martina Sellmeyer's memorial book. But in July 2015, the celebrated feminist, aged 78, decided to visit after all, again as a guest of the city.[39] By then, Hélène's mother was no longer living, having died two years earlier. In Hélène's memory – "which is perhaps a screen memory" – Osnabrück was imprinted as "a ravishing little city."[40] "Impossible to go there without the help of phantasms."[41]

Perhaps among all the unknown reasons for going to Osnabrück, where good and evil grow together on the apple tree, I had wanted to see where, in what décor, in which streets, in what music of language my mother's life, and subsequently mine, had begun to be interpellated, declared, then convoked by the word Jew, where, in what landscape, in what climate, on what occasion, or date or season, I had lost, before my birth, rights: the rights of the self, the right to be-Jewish and to be-notJewish at will, at my will, according to my desire, whenever I felt like it. … I was going there as a Jew

---

37. Cixous, *Osnabrück Station*, 67–68. German and English in the original.
38. Ibid., 14.
39. "Toute de suite après elle publie *Gare d'Osnabrück à Jérusalem* et *Correspondance avec le Mur*, livres qui célèbrent Osnabrück et Jérusalem comme villes mythiques, promises, mais dont le retour est toujours differé. Ajoutons a cette série *Une autobiographie allemande*, livre d'entretiens avec Cecile Wajsbrot, et *Ruines bien rangés*: on est déjà au septième livre de ce que l'autrice appelle désormais ses 'Contes et légends d'Osnabrück." Christa Stevens, LIEJ – Littérature et Judéité. "'Les plis noir de la grande tragedie': sur *Gare d'Osnabrück à Jerusalem* d'Hélène Cixous." https://liej.hypotheses.org /christa-stevens. Among other things, Stevens' article delves into the Jewish aspects of Cixous' *Osnabrück*.
40. Cisoux, *Osnabrück Station*, 13.
41. Ibid., 9.

and also as non-Jew, I represented the two complementary aspects, thus as Jew-it-depends, as woman and daughter and also Jew as daughter of my mother from Osnabrück"…. [T]he right not to hide that, in front of the apple of pity and cruelty, every human is equal to every human being so long as she/he has not made her/his choice.[42]

In 2015, notes Cisoux, there were 192 *Stolpersteine* ("stumbling stones") laid out in Osnabrück, each one inscribed with the name, date of birth and fate of a victim of Nazi persecution and annihilation.

ERICH MARIA REMARQUE

Towards the end of *The Black Obelisk,* Erich Maria Remarque's novel set against the backdrop of the Great Inflation of 1923/24, the author runs down the fate of those who served the Nazi regime in Werden-brück (read: Osnabrück) and beyond. In fiction as in real life, Remarque's Nazis wound up with good jobs, "distinguished careers," and generous pensions.

The same holds for Remarque's 1958 war novel *Der Funke Leben* (*Spark of Life*). Tim Westphalen's afterword laments the exoneration of Nazi perpetrators, their enrichment at the expense of the victims, and effortless resumption of their careers in the postwar Federal Republic of Germany.[43]

Der Funke Leben is dedicated to the memory of Remarque's sister Elfriede Scholz (née Remark). Accused of sabotaging the war effort, Elfriede was sentenced to death by Roland Freisler, the same that took the lives of Sophie and Hans Scholl and their "co-conspirators." Today Osnabrück has a street after Elfriede Scholz. Hélène Cixous:

> thus by myriad vicious offences, violence, still smarting cruelties, the entire city was forever profaned and poisoned for Remarque – take one concrete example: should he walk down Elfriede-Scholz

42. Ibid., 117–118. Cited as written.
43. Nachwort von Tilman Westphalen, "Die Würde des Menschen ist unantastbar," in Erich Maria Remarque, *Der Funke Leben* (Köln: Kiepenheuer & Witsch, 1998), 384.

Street, that is walk on his sister's body, with or without her head, or avoid it? – make a speech about the victims of torture metamorphosed into streets or squares? One can't remain silent, one must remain silent[44]

Freisler died in February 1945. In 1985, his widow learned that her war widow's pension had been augmented by a monthly 400 RM. The increase was based on her deceased husband's potential earnings in the Federal Republic as a "lawyer or civil servant in the higher echelons."[45]

In a 1944 memorandum Remarque prepared for the US Secret Service, "Praktische Erziehungsarbeit in Deutschland nach dem Krieg" ("Practical Educational Work in Germany After the War"), the author of *All Quiet on the Western Front* advocated an unsparing confrontation with Nazi crimes: concentration camps in Germany and in the occupied territories; shooting of hostages; murder of civilians; systematic murder of Jews; theft, murder, expropriation and "Aryanization," and other treacherously secured property, and so forth. Like Georg Hermann, Remarque flayed 60,000,000 Germans for their "scandalous persecution of 500,000 Jews." A key point is the demand that war criminals "be held accountable with more stringent and greater outrage than any Allied Court could ever muster."[46]

"The complete works of Remarque," states the official website of Osnabrück's Erich Maria Remarque Peace Center, "form an integral part of his Osnabrück background and offer a critical examination of German history, whereby the preservation of human dignity and humanity in times of oppression, terror, and war always stood at the forefront of his literary creation. Remarque is therefore widely regarded as a credible representative of the 'other Germany.'"[47]

---

44. Cixous, *Well-Kept Ruins*, 52.
45. Tilman-Westphalen, Nachwort, 389.
46. Ibid., 390–391.
47. https://www.remarque.uni-osnabrueck.de

FELIX NUSSBAUM

Designed by Daniel Libeskind, the Felix Nussbaum Haus was inaugurated in 1998 and houses some 200 works by the murdered artist.

On May 10, 1940, the German armies swept into the Netherlands, Belgium, Luxemburg, and France. As a German national, albeit a refugee, Felix was arrested in Brussels and interned in Camp Saint-Cyprien on the Mediterranean coast. On August 3, Felix signed a paper requesting return to Germany, in compliance with a Vichy decree repatriating all war and civil internees to the Reich. As a Jew, Felix didn't qualify, however. He and Georg Meyer, a former schoolmate from Osnabrück, managed to escape to Bordeaux, where they were put up in a barracks.

Georg Meyer:

> Felix Nussbaum got scared and wanted to go back to the barracks. I told him that then we would be shot. We took a bus to a suburb to find a train. There were only military transports. The stationmaster seemed to understand our situation and let us stay (for a fee) the night in a Red Cross train. Soon afterwards German soldiers came

for control. In the next compartment people were arrested and taken away, and in the general excitement our compartment was overlooked. This is how we got to the Gare de Midi in Brussels.… In 1945 I learned from friends that Felix had been denounced and deported.[48]

Felix Nussbaum reached the age of 39.

KADDISH FOR FELIX NUSSBAUM (1904–1944)

…

So sorry for myself
while you were behind electrified
barbed wire in St. Cyprien,
either sweltering in cement barracks
or scorched, the sun never
ceasing its beating,
you sleeping on sand and straw,
your plate a tin can. But somehow you kept painting
tallised men entering a makeshift synagogue,
their backs to the horror and yourself
surrounded by walls impossible to climb,
wearing the yellow star on your coat
and holding a Jewish identity card;
so I could go to Chattanooga on leave,
dance the lindy with *sheigitz* boys,
eat a B.L.T. for the first time
and visit a plastic surgeon
to have my nose made non-Jewish,
small and turned-up.[49]

* * *

---

48. Cited in Junk and Sellmeyer, *Stationen*, 160.

49. Excerpt from "Kaddish For Felix Nussbaum (1904–1944)," a poem by Oregon poet Willa Schneberg, previously published in the anthology *Beyond Lament: Poets of the World Bearing Witness to the Holocaust*, edited

Chapter V
Writers Guild

The Occupation was merciless in exposing character.[1]
– Frederic Spotts

Everything we did was equivocal. We never quite knew whether we were doing right or wrong. A subtle poison corrupted even our best actions.[2]
– Jean-Paul Sartre

A train filled with Jews surges through my mind, I throw the switch and reroute the past.[3]
– Bert Voeten

1. The Kindest Man

I've decided to end my life. I'm done. I made that decision some thirty years ago – that's how long I've been thinking about it, creating a sense of invulnerability for myself. . . . I knew it all along: I'll

---

by Marguerite M. Striar (Evanston, Illinois: Northwestern University Press, 1998), and *In the Margins of the World* (Austin, Texas: Plain View Press, 2001).
1. Frederic Spotts, *The Shameful Peace: How French Artists and Intellectuals Survived the Nazi Occupation* (New Haven, CT: Yale University Press, 2008), 256.
2. Ibid., 4.
3. "Er rijdt door mijn hoofd een trein/vol joden, ik leg het verleden/als een wissel om." *De trein* (1954), poem, https://www.dbnl.org/tekst/_gid001195401 _01/_gid001195401_01_0135.php (accessed January 10, 2023).

live to around fifty. Being a writer has been a central part of my life. As a writer, I have achieved part of what I set out to do: the part involving research and journalism, the non-fiction aspect. That part I consider successful; moreover, that type of work increasingly shaped my worldview. Fiction gradually receded into the background because I couldn't live up to the standard I had set for myself, which accounts for 20% of my disappointment…. The immersion in journalism quickly filled the gap, trumping fiction with writing that is better than that of many a professional historian. This was how the commitment to research gradually took hold, sustained by tenacity, rage, determination, and the conviction to speak my mind, even at great personal risk and regardless of the fallout.[4]

Adriaan Venema, born May 27, 1941, committed suicide on October 31, 1993, aged 52, overdosing on barbiturates, in the presence of his wife and youngest son. His wife, whom he known since 1989 and married several weeks before his death, said he was the kindest man she'd ever known. "He was afraid of deteriorating and going down in one fell swoop. He couldn't deal with that. That's why he killed himself."[5]

4. Ischa Meijer, *De interviewer en de schrijvers* (The interviewer and the writers), https://www.dbnl.org/tekst/meijo12inteo4_01/meijo12inteo4_01_0017.php, 334–39. The interview took place on September 3, 1991.
5. *Leeuwarder Courant,* January 26, 1994.

2. A Sharp Eye for the Telling Detail

The Netherlands' Lucy B. and C.W. van der Hoogtprijs is a prestigious literary prize awarded annually. In 1947, the award went to Bert Voeten, for *Doortocht* (Passage), a wartime diary covering the years of occupation, May 1940 to May 1945. "Amid the stream of wartime diaries and resistance literature published this past year," wrote a reviewer in a major Dutch newspaper, "*Doortocht* by the young poet Bert Voeten doubtlessly belongs to the best books about the war and occupation hitherto published. With a sharp eye for the telling detail, Bert Voeten's 200-plus pages offer a solid, well-rounded chronological overview, literature rather than journalism. The imprint of the writer's personality distinguishes it from a mere journalistic account."[6]

Bert Voeten died December 26, 1992, aged 74. "Voeten," memorialized Amsterdam newspaper *Het Parool*,

> was a sensitive observer of reality.... In addition to poetry, Voeten was known for his translations of German, French, and English plays, especially Shakespeare's. The diary turned out to be Voeten's only notable prose work. Towards the end of the 1980s, Voeten was discredited when Adriaan Venema... contended that his wartime diary was a fake – passages had not been written on the day recorded – and that Voeten had concealed that during the war he had worked as a correspondent for the Nazi Chamber of Culture, accusations Venema would subsequently repeat in his study *Schrijvers, uitgevers en hun collaboratie* [Writers, publishers, and their collaboration]. Voeten denied that his diary was a forgery but did admit to having briefly worked for the Cultural Chamber. Voeten: 'I was incapable of owning up to this before. I can't figure out why, I must've repressed it.'

"Voeten," the article concluded, "having temporarily lost his way, subsequently helped many Jews find hiding places. One of these was Marga Minco. They married in 1944. Bert Voeten is to be buried today, amid family."[7]

---

6. *Algemeen Handelsblad*, October 21, 1946.
7. December 30, 1992. As for helping other Jews find hiding places, the record

Introduced in November 1941 and modelled after the German prototype, the Chamber of Culture was to "coordinate" – i.e., Nazify – Holland's cultural, educational, and intellectual life. The entire arts sector was incorporated into the Department for Popular Enlightenment and the Arts.[8] To publish, writers had to sign off on the Cultural Chamber and the Aryan Declaration. Jews and communists were excluded. Overseeing the Chamber was Professor Tobi Goedewagen, philosopher, poet, and ardent National Socialist. The fact that the professor owed his appointment to Arthur Seyss-Inquart, Reichskommissar for the Occupied Netherlands, indicates that the imposition of a Nazi-style cultural straitjacket was no mere afterthought but a crucial component of the country's projected integration into a Greater German Reich. The Cultural Chamber allocated subsidies and awarded literary prizes "in the hope of promoting writing for the New Order." The Chamber engaged "correspondents" to spread the word, recruit new members, and assess the mood among writers and artists. Voeten was the Chamber's emissary for southern Holland, where he lived and worked. In 1943 Voeten quit the Cultural Chamber and moved to Amsterdam.

3. DON'T JOIN THE GUILDS!

From the very beginning, opponents of the Chamber sounded the alarm and implored writers, artists, and intellectuals to boycott the various guilds incorporating their specific métier. "Writers, painters, sculptors, musicians, artisans, architects…know what you're doing; by choosing the Cultural Chamber over your HONOR AS ARTIST you are forfeiting the right to serve the arts. Your moment has arrived: total war forces you to speak out and take a stand: FOR OR AGAINST FASCISM; FOR OR AGAINST ENSLAVEMENT, MURDER, AND SUSPENSION OF JUSTICE! FOR OR AGAINST THE GERMAN WORLD CONQUEROR! FOR OR AGAINST…THE BEAUTY OF THE ARTS. Dutch Artists: Defy

---

is inconclusive. For Minco, also see Chapter 1, fn. 18. Minco died July 10, 2023, aged 103.

8. DVK: Departement van Volksvoorlichting en Kunsten (Department of Popular Enlightenment and the Arts).

threats, bribery, and material hardships... do not underestimate the immense significance of a powerful 'NO' by the collectivity of Dutch artists. DON'T JOIN THE GUILDS! And reduce the announcement of the Cultural Chamber to an empty gesture by these Nazi buffoons."[9]

Adriaan Venema's *Het systeem* (1988), the first of five volumes tracking the collaboration of writers and publishers under German occupation, makes the case against Bert Voeten: his involvement with the Cultural Chamber, penning fascist-inspired poetry, and, above all, for passing off his wartime diary as the genuine article.[10]

---

9. *Rebel, mijn hart: kunstenaars 1940–45* (Rebel, my heart: artist 1940–45) (Zwolle: Uitgeverij Waanders, 1995), 41.
10. *Schrijvers, uitgevers en hun collaboratie, 1: het system* (Amsterdam, Arbeiderspers, 1988).

"The story," Venema writes in the introduction to that first volume, "begins in the May days of 1940, on the day (Holland's) capitulation made the German occupation a fact. From that moment forward everyone was confronted with the choice of whether to reject or accept the occupier's ideology, and if the latter, to what degree." Bad enough that writers like Voeten had "forfeited the right to serve the arts." The fact that after 1945 they should try to cover it up, Venema found equally, if not more, reprehensible. For writers, being writers, were best equipped "to write their own history and falsify it." Collaborating writers continued to write after the war as though they were on the same page with those who had refused to join the Cultural Chamber and suffered the consequences.[11] Few were held accountable, penalties were rare and mild, a short-term publishing ban being one. "The prevailing image is that writers by and large resisted, people who stood up for their convictions and would have no truck with National Socialism. When I questioned this image, all hell broke loose."[12]

Venema charts the method and the mission, the what and the why. While the method hewed to conventional historical practices, grounded in primary and secondary sources, the mission injected moral and ethical norms. There would be no pretense of objectivity, of what is ordinarily understood by objectivity or impartiality. Venema made no bones about it: "Writers, publishers, and their collaboration" was, unavoidably, a polemic. Collaborators deserved nothing less. As Venema saw it, the facts did speak for themselves, so why split hairs? Case in point: Voeten's diary – a "sophisticated lie," a cover-up for having worked for the Nazis. Full stop. As for the style, Venema agreed with an early critic who characterized the writing as a sophisticated amalgam of hollow phrases, culled with an eye on "the way people liked to think of themselves, depriving the diary of much of the value it might have had."[13]

---

11. Venema, *Verleden tijd: Memoires* (Past Tense: Memoirs) (Amsterdam: Uitgeverij Balans, 1994), 23.

12. Ibid., 253.

13. W.F. Hermans, cited in Venema, *Writers* vol 1, 285. Hermans registered with the Cultural Chamber on August 26, 1942, but kept quiet about it, having

Voeten, contended Venema, "turned into an avid propagandist for the Cultural Chamber." The reports correspondents filed at the end of each month proved as much. Voeten started "winning souls" (Voeten's words) on its behalf from the get-go, talking up the benefits of belonging to "an organization devoted to the general improvement of the socio-economic position of artists without impeding the free development of the artistic impulse." These reports, Venema emphasized, were no mere formalities. The correspondent was a spy, knowing full well that the higher-ups would be able to use the information against the vacillators. Why, asks Venema, did Voeten choose to become a correspondent rather than follow the example of scores of writers and artists who registered with the Cultural Chamber and let it go at that? Because: "He wanted more: to recruit members and help spread 'the great revolution.'" "In itself, the fact that a person entertains vastly different ideas in a diary from those aired in a monthly report is of little importance," observed Venema. "Here, however, we are dealing with an attempt to influence historiography itself. The bestowal of an important award transformed it into to 'a literary monument' and, ipso facto, an important contribution to our knowledge about the occupation.... What is recorded in a diary should be true."

4. "Sing, Battering Ram, Sing!"

Between 1940 and 1943, Voeten contributed 38 poems to *Aristo*, an antisemitic, fascist journal. "Song of the Battering Ram"[14] is typical. The battering ram beats against the gates of fossilized town walls;

---

earlier signed the loyalty oath required of civil servants in higher education and the civil service. See Dirk Baartse, "Kultuurkamergeleerde," (Cultural Chamber Scholar), in *De God van Nederland ziet alles!* (The God of the Netherlands sees all), January–March 2014, No. 10, 38–39. The satirical magazine ceased publication several years ago. Hermans would go on to become one of Holland's foremost writers.

14. "Lied van den stormram" appeared in *Aristo* in February 1941. *Aristo* folded in 1943. See Bijlage XI (Supplement), *Het Systeem*, 511–12. *Zing maar, stormram/zing,/dreun uw lied/ op de poorten/der verstikten steden.../want wij willen leven,/groots en heftig....*

spirits awaken; fists unclench; eyes open; bodies stretch; streets resound with strident voices yearning to live passionately, ferociously; joyful fires salute the new. "Sing, battering ram!"

Venema points to the discrepancy between a poem in a fascist magazine that sings the praises of the new dispensation on the one hand, appropriating the language of the Third Reich, and the diary's unequivocal condemnation of antisemitism and the occupier's persecution of the Jews on the other. "We should not fail to mention," Venema concludes,

> that at the end of 1943, thus after his *Aristo* venture, Voeten came to his senses. Mussolini had fallen, and with the defeat of Germany assured, he must have realized that, however belatedly, the time had come for a decisive about-face. He broke off all contacts with his seducers and went into hiding. Undoubtedly, the writer Marga Minco owes her life to his protection, an act against which much of what he had done previously sinks into insignificance.

How to judge someone like Voeten? The answer, Venema says, lies with the admission of guilt as "the sole righteous criterion in dispensing forgiveness and leniency… because it comes down to the recognition of… a society grounded in norms, on values that have general validity and bring no harm to the community."[15] Given its assumed credibility as a reliable historical source, Voeten's backdated diary, Venema found, did harm society and the values on which it rests.

5. Playing God

"The good judge, whatever his secret heart desires," observed French historian Marc Bloch in *The Historian's Craft*, "questions witnesses with no other concern than

> to know the facts, whatever they may be. For both [judge and scholar] this is an obligation of conscience which is never ques-

15. The words cited by Venema are from a 1954 speech by Victor van Vriesland at the biennial awards ceremony of the Foundation Artists' Resistance 1942–1945. Van Vriesland was a Jewish author who spent the war years in hiding.

tioned. However, there comes a moment when their paths divide. When the scholar has observed and explained, his task is finished. It yet remains for the judge to pass sentence. If, imposing silence on his personal inclination, he pronounces it according to the law, he will be deemed impartial. And he will be impartial in a judicial sense, not in a scientific sense. For we can neither condemn nor absolve without accepting a table of values which no longer refers to any positive science. That one man has killed another is a fact which is eminently susceptible of proof. But to punish the murderer assumes that we consider murder culpable: which is, after all, only an opinion about which not all civilizations have agreed.

"We all play God in judging," concludes the historian, citing Pascal: "this is good or this is evil."

Men forget that a value judgment has a raison d'être only as preparation for an action and a meaning solely in relation to a system of consciously accepted moral references. When the passions of the past blend with the prejudices of the present, human reality is reduced to a picture of black and white.... To round off, 'understanding,' is the beacon light of our studies."[16]

Venema's revelations in *The System* and subsequent volumes did not sit well with the critics, to put it mildly.[17] Unlike Bloch, Venema didn't think his task was finished once he had "observed and explained." If only things were that simple! Venema's critics – better put: his detractors – were not impressed. The overwhelming majority took a battering ram to the author: Venema was a "psychopath," "a troubled individual," "nitpicker," "maniac," "possessed," "muckraker," "destroyer

16. Marc Bloch, *The Historian's Craft*. Trans. from the French (*Apologie pour l'histoire*) by Peter Putnam (New York, Vintage Books, 1953), 139–140, 143. Bloch joined the French resistance and was executed in 1944.
17. "Reacties," in *Uitgevers en boekhandelaren* (Publishers and booksellers), Vol. 4, 1992, 447–469.
https://www.dbnl.org/tekst/vene001schr05_01/vene001schr05_01_0008 .php.

of reputations," "crazy," "inquisitor," "soulless and disrespectful," "a manhunter," and "a pimp who turned in his own whores."

Such terminology, responded Venema, smacked of National Socialist propaganda and Stalinist invective. Hard-headed and opiniated he was, Venema conceded, and his manner off-putting, but what of it? "I don't agonize about the number of enemies I make because of the positions I take."[18] "Whatever they may say about my work, the facts check out."[19] Sure enough, Venema's critics found little to complain about on that head: he had done his homework. What troubled them was the self-styled historian's presumptuous trifecta: scholar, judge, and executioner rolled into one, the conclusions he drew and their brazen presentation.

In 1986, Venema, a former art dealer, wrote a book about the wartime art market, likewise centered on collaboration.[20] Two years later, Venema was accused of financing fake Karel Appel lithographs. He denied it, albeit without the customary surefootedness, leaving a gray area of doubt. A taste of his own medicine, his enemies rejoiced. "As though," Venema responded, "selling looted Jewish property is comparable to selling fake Appel lithographs, if indeed I had done so."[21]

6. The Gray Past

Eight years after Venema's death in 1993, Dutch historian Chris van der Heijden came out with *Grijs verleden: Nederland en de Tweede Wereldoorlog*[22] (The gray past: the Netherlands and the Second World War). Van der Heijden's study took issue with labeling wartime's citizenry as either "good" or "bad," those who fought back ("goed") and those who collaborated ("fout)." The reality, Van der Heijden

---

18. *Blommeldingen* (Amsterdam, Gerard Timmer Prods: 1990), 90.
19. Venema, *Verleden tijd*, 158.
20. *Kunsthandel in Nederland 1940–45.*
21. Venema, *Verleden tijd*, 223.
22. *Grijs verleden: Nederland en de Tweede Wereldoorlog* (Amsterdam/Antwerpen: Uitgeverij Contact, 2001). Alternative meanings of "goed" and "fout": "right" and "wrong"; "black and white."

argued, was rather more complicated – "gray," denoting that the truth lay somewhere in the middle.

Van der Heijden devoted an entire chapter to Venema's findings. "Uproar Round Good and Bad" argued that the author's biases did little to promote understanding. He attributed a good deal of the negative reaction to Venema's magnum opus to his character." "Born in 1941," he writes,

> and thus part of the first generation that had few or no memories of the war, towards the end of the sixties he became part of the capital's journalistic, literary, and art scene. In each of these circumscribed worlds he never failed to attract attention, not so much by virtue of his talent as his venomous tongue and vicious pen. If this proved to be financially damaging to his art dealership, in literature and journalism it earned him, at best, the reputation of *enfant terrible*, at worst that of a charlatan . . . a type close to Venema's heart.[23]

In 1961, Van der Heijden related, some of Holland's leading public intellectuals convened in Amsterdam to discuss Holland's role in the destruction of their Jews. Titled "Eichmann Was Not Alone," the gathering included the "postwar icon of Jewish suffering," Marga Minco.[24] "Without the assistance of the Dutch police, the civil servants, railway personnel and the citizenry that looked the other way," wrote Van der Heijden summarizing their conclusions, "none of it would have happened. The tone for the trauma was set."[25]

In the latter half of the 1960s, he added, "the war became increasingly associated with the Jewish drama." Van der Heijden singled out one book above all for precipitating this dramatic shift: Jacques Presser's *The Destruction of the Dutch Jews*.[26] Professor Presser's book came out in 1965 and hit Holland like a bomb, stirring up repressed feelings

---

23. Ibid, 375–76.
24. Ibid., 374.
25. Ibid., 377
26. *Ondergang: De vervolging en verdelging van het Nederlandse Jodendom 1940–1945* ('s-Gravenhage: Staatsuitgeverij, 1965). *The Destruction of the Dutch*

of guilt. Presser's history was nothing if not "engaged"; Presser's wife had died in a concentration camp and Presser himself spent two years in hiding. His two-volume opus came down hard on the Dutch and their failure to stand by their Auschwitz-bound Jewish compatriots. Van der Heijden:

> The consequences were enormous. All at once everyone who during the occupation was not in the resistance or in London [seat of the government in exile] was guilty or felt himself such. And everyone who had the slightest contact with the Germans was a murderer or accomplice.… they all had blood on their hands.… Around 1970, Adriaan Venema was one of the young ones for whom 'the war' became the frame of reference par excellence.… Friendship was determined by whether someone could be trusted to provide you with a place to hide.… One was for or against, compromise was out of the question.… The five-volume series on the collaboration of writers and publishers marked the nadir of Venema's obsession with the war: 'a stunt'.… [I]n his person and work Venema represented a corrupt version of a Dutch phenomenon.[27]

For all that, Van der Heijden acknowledged that Venema's "obsession" was hardly that of a madman; if so, it wouldn't have kicked up the fuss it did – nor worthy of an entire chapter by a professional historian.

7. Good, Bad, Indifferent

Granted, Venema's framework is more than a tad simplistic, the terminology loaded. The very construct raises intractable obstacles. Where, on a collaboration scale of one to ten, does one place the individual who signed off on the plunder of Jewish household goods? The driver of the van who transported the loot to a warehouse? The average citizen who looked the other way as Jews were being carted

---

Jews, trans. Arnold Pomerans (New York, E.P. Dutton, Inc., 1969). Alternative English title: *Ashes in the Wind*. For Presser, see Chapter VI.

27. Van der Heijden, *Grijs verleden*, 379, 386.

off under their very noses? The Dutch police that helped round up Jews? The writers, journalists, and civil servants who signed off on the Aryan Declaration? The answer remains elusive. That Germany would lose the war was no foregone conclusion. The occupation became a fact of everyday life and the incorporation of the Netherlands into a Greater German Reich a real possibility. The price of active resistance could mean death. It was not uncommon for families to split along *goed/fout*, "good" vs. "bad." Van der Heijden's parents were active members of the Dutch Nazi Party; the historian's father joined the Waffen SS, the combat branch of the SS. The paternal grandparents of Professor J.C.H. Blom, the former director of The Netherlands Institute for War Documentation and Genocide Studies, were ardent Nazis; a son, however, was in the resistance. Venema's grandmother was a known collaborator.

Black and white, good and bad, right and wrong, things were quite a bit simpler during the war. Or were they? For the perplexed, there was the underground press to set them straight. One such, Amsterdam's *Het Parool*, published an article in October 1943 demarcating the fault lines between "good" and "bad." Headlined "Oh, We Dutch are 'so good.' But…When are you *really* 'good'?"[28] the paper scoffed at the prevailing opinion the Dutch had of themselves as being overwhelmingly "good." Well, yes, 100,000 bad apples, i.e., N.S.B. – "scum, misfits, and adventurers," "dregs of the nation" – but what about the rest? Many of the latter think of themselves as upright, decent patriots. But are they therefore "good?" The article compared the conduct of the Dutch in a variety of situations with those of other occupied nations without, however, distinguishing between occupation policies, types of regime (military or civilian), and "racial" composition. Nazi racial theory considered the Dutch "Aryans," Slavs like Russians and Poles subhuman, "life unworthy of life."[29] Norwegian women gave German

---

28. "O, wij Nederanders zijn zo 'good'; Maar…Wanneeer ben je dan eigenlijk "goed?" In *De Jaren '40–'45* Rijksinstituut voor oorlogsdocumentatie (1961), 188.
29. Belgium and France, for example, had a German military government. Holland was treated as a protectorate, a non-incorporated territory of the Reich, giving the SS a free hand in implementing anti-Jewish decrees. Norway

soldiers the cold shoulder, Dutch women had babies by them. Belgium judges had refused to cooperate, Holland's Supreme Court went along for the ride. In Holland, German films drew huge audiences. In Poland, the people stayed away. In France, German trains had been derailed, while Holland's railways helped transport Jews to transit camp Westerbork and on to the death camps in Poland. The country's highest civil servants exported goods and workers to Germany, lunched with the enemy, and even entertained them in their homes. The press pretended to be "good" but continued to spread German lies, albeit under "pressure and coordination." In the meantime, press lords made money hand over fist. People say they were opposed to the Dutch Nazi Party but shunned resistance like the plague because it was deemed "illegal."

The masses, the article chided, sheepishly complied with every German decree. They turned in the Aryan Declaration and their radios on the double, so much so, the paper related, that Reichskommissar Arthur Seyss-Inquart expressed surprise at the eagerness with which the Dutch heeded summons after summons. "But the Dutch people are 'good!' And we won't knuckle under. In the meantime, N.S.B thugs were murdering our citizens, three for every one of theirs, and still walking around scot-free." Finally, the paper offered some guidelines to help their compatriots get a grip.

> In this struggle, only they are "good" whose every action is governed by the notion of how to inflict the most damage on the occupier and their henchmen. Only they are "good" who actively help to find hiding places for those in need; who help spread illegal writing; who help derail trains; who participate in setting fire to factories that work for the German war machine; who help promote anti-German spying, and in a thousand other ways contributes to bringing down the Nazi system in the shortest possible time. Only they are good who minimizes cooperation and maximizes

had a pro-German government headed by Vidkun Quisling. Unlike the Dutch, Poles were considered *Untermenschen,* and treated as such; as many Polish non-Jews were murdered as Polish Jews: 3,000,000.

opposition.... Whoever can't do that, or doesn't want or dare to, is part of the passive, indifferent, inert masses. That's the only "good" thing we can say about them.

Bert Voeten sheltered his Jewish girlfriend Marga Minco, an act Venema held to have virtually erased his sins of omission and commission. That was to the *goed*. In his memoir, Venema claimed never to have said that Voeten was an out-and-out collaborator, but that he and his ilk were "cardsharps," "cheaters."[30]

8. *The Diary*, the Novel

Several critics noted that Venema was in no position to judge because he wasn't there. "Which is like asking a historian whether, under similar circumstances, he would have acted any different from a historical character he'd been investigating," rejoined Venema. "Is the literary critic required to write a novel that is better than the work he put down in a review?"[31]

Speaking of novels: in 1991, Venema said that he gave up writing fiction because he couldn't live up to the standard he had set for himself. The bar must've been set rather high because *Het dagboek* (The diary), Venema's fictionalized account of the Voeten affair, is a good read. It also is subtler and far kinder to its protagonist than the non-fiction precursor. In his posthumously published memoir Venema described his rationale for writing it, as well as some of the critical fallout, as follows:

> The novel *Het dagboek* is a typical example of a novel about real-life events packaged as fiction. The protagonist, called Engel [Angel], of course is Bert Voeten. It is about a man who practiced deception during the war and at the end of the war contrived a diary in which he becomes a resistance hero. The book is about the fears he endured because he knew the secret would one day come out. Why

---

30. *Verleden tijd*, 265. The word Venema used is "sjoemelaars."
31. Venema dealt with the objections to his study in Appendix VII of Volume 4, "Reacties."

did I write this novel? A lot of people were furious. They accused me of piling on. Some reviews were in the same vein. I don't agree. I found Bert Voeten and his conduct during and after the war to be an ideal subject. What's more, preoccupied with collaborating writers as I was, I felt an irrepressible urge to give this theme a literary form. Bert Voeten should have written that book, and I said so in in several interviews. But he didn't. He never spoke publicly about his motives and that piqued my curiosity. That's why I tried to understand Bert Voeten and others like him who at times failed during the war and made up a story afterwards.... I saw reviews with headlines such as: "Novel as a License to Commit Character Assassination"; "Wretched Novel by 'Hunter' Adriaan Venema"; "*Het dagboek*, Venema's Mushy Roman à clef."[32]

The novel is divided into two parts, *De rijdende trein – The moving train* – and *De sprong naar voren – the leap forward*. The former is the train that drags Engel along the path of small-bore collaboration – until it doesn't. Part 2 describes Engel's evolution toward wholeness as well as the repercussions attendant upon the exposure of the diary as bogus.

The novel opens in the late 1940s. Engel's wartime diary has catapulted him to fame. He sits on literary juries and committees, disbursing awards and prizes and is much in demand as a speaker, especially at gatherings memorializing the occupation. On one such occasion, a wartime acquaintance and fellow poet with a checkered past not unlike Engel's gives a speech and Engel reads a couple of poems. We are playing with fire, he tells Engel. "You and I are in the same boat."

Venema, of course, holds the master key, opening this, then that door. One door leads to Ine, Engel's girlfriend. Jewish, Ine was fired from her job at the newspaper that also employed Engel; no one protested. The paper was not to weigh in on anti-Jewish measures. To avoid capture and deportation, Ine keeps a low profile. Another door opens onto Voeten's soul-searching; after all, he never was a Nazi, certified or otherwise. In Venema's telling, Engel-Voeten comes

32. Venema, *Verleden tijd*, 285–86.

across as naïve, easily impressed – "managed" – deluding himself that as a correspondent for the Cultural Chamber he could bore from within. Dispatched to gauge the mood at an artists' meeting, a sculptor remarks: "You go from door to door like a traveling salesman with a product in which you don't really believe. That's worse than the N.S.B."

Part 2, *The leap forward*. New Year's Day 1944. German defeat looms. By now Engel has quit the newspaper and the Cultural Chamber; *Aristo* has folded. In March 1944, Engel cut the remaining ties with his past and tested the waters of the resistance. The last of the Jews had been deported or gone into hiding. He concocts the fake diary and at war's end submits it to a publisher.

One day, the publisher tells him that the Military Authority had a file on him and that he had been fingered for "cleansing." The cleansing agent is a literary tribunal called into existence to interrogate suspected collaborators. If convicted, there would be no publication and the advance would have to be paid back. Engel denied the charges, including being a correspondent. Conveniently, for Engel, that is, the most important witness had died on the Eastern front. Engel pulls out his ace in the hole. Ine writes a letter testifying to her savior's "goodness." This proved decisive. The tribunal still had its doubts but nonetheless lets him off the hook. Nothing now stands in the way of accepting Netherlands' prestigious literary award, the Lucy B. and C. van der Hoogt Prize.

Years later, Engel runs into one of the tribunal's jurors on a park bench. This juror knew all along that Engel had deceived the tribunal. "It is your life, as it was your choice to lie to us," he says. "At the time, I already knew that you would be tormented by terrible fears. . . . All things considered, what you did wasn't so terrible that after all these years you should still be startled every time the telephone rings or your mailbox clatters shut. You've been punished enough already." "I was bad," says Engel. "I lied to everyone." "Bad? No, not dumb, just stupid. I hope," the former juror says in parting, "that you get that call soon, and at last get it over and done with."

Back home, Engel tells Ine about his encounter and the juror's name. Flabbergasted, Ine responds: "But that guy has been dead for years!"

Regarding the ending, one reviewer wrote:

[T]he novel…is well written, and especially the ending. The conclusion, however, is cruel. Because Venema runs the show, he can afford to be compassionate. But since he is the one who drew attention to Voeten's involvement with the Cultural Chamber in the first place, his sympathy comes across as phony. Had he written the novel Venema has, Voeten surely would have received the Lucy B. and C.W. van der Hoogt Prize, albeit for literature.[33]

9. Primal Scream

Venema's memoir *Verleden tijd*, a score-settling exercise in self-justification and vengeance that all-too-often defaults to a diatribe, came out in 1993, a year after the author's death by suicide. In his 52 years Venema had made a lot of enemies, so there was a lot to attend to.

The memoir starts out with a brutal assault in the parking lot of a radio station where he was about to be interviewed. The interview concerned the publication of a memoir by the widow of Dutch National Socialist Leader Rost van Tonningen, second in command to N.S.B. chief Anton Mussert, a hardened SS stalwart and Nazi collaborator par excellence. Rost van Tonningen died in 1945, whether by his own hand or murdered is unclear.

The date of the interview was November 14, 1990. Getting out of his car, Venema was brutally assaulted by two men who went straight for his head.

I once read that if attacked and it is impossible to defend yourself that you should raise your knees and hold your hands on top of your head in a sort of fetal position. That's what I did instinctively. They dashed forward and had me by the legs before I could shut

---

33. Hans Renders, "Adriaan Venema: Het dagboek. Een roman over '40–'45" (Adriaan Venema: The diary. A novel about '40–'45). NRC *Handelsblad*, March 23, 1993.

the door. I grabbed the steering wheel and tried to stop them from pulling me out of the car, but they were too strong. They dragged me out of the car, and I hit the ground. The smaller of the two hit me with a blackjack, the bigger one with a baseball bat. They hit my hands with all their might to get them off my head, but I kept protecting my head. They then kicked and punched my ribs, again trying to get me to lower my arms. But I didn't, regardless of the pain. All I did was scream as loud as I could.[34]

AAAAAAAAAAAAAAAAAAAAAAAAAAAAAAAAAAAAAAAAAAAAAA
AAAAAAAAAAAAAAAAAAAAAAAAAAAAAAAAAAAAAAAAAAAAAA
AAAAAAAAAAAAAAAAAAAAAAAAAAAAAAAAAAAAAAAAAAAAAA

*   *   *

---

34. *Verleden tijd*, 25–26.

Chapter VI
The Historian

Schreibe mit Blut, and du wirst erfahren, dass Blut Geist ist –
Write with blood, and thou wilt find that blood is spirit.

– Friedrich Nietzsche

1. Interview with Philo Bregstein

In the fall of 1986, I interviewed Dutch writer and filmmaker Philo Bregstein. Bregstein was in San Francisco as the guest of the Jewish Film Festival, which showed three of his documentaries: *The Past That Lives*, featuring Dutch-Jewish historian Jacques Presser; *Long Journey Through His Times*, a biography of the German-Jewish conductor Otto Klemperer, and *In Search of Jewish Amsterdam*, depicting Jewish life in pre-war Amsterdam.

I started out by asking Mr. Bregstein whether he considered himself a Jewish filmmaker.

Am I a Jewish filmmaker, that is, do I make exclusively Jewish films? No. I have made films about a Swiss painter, a Dutch novelist, a French anthropologist, as well as a regular feature film. But I will say this: my interest in making Jewish films, films about Jews stems from a personal quest for self-knowledge, a journey inward, an ongoing attempt to come to grips with my past, as well as with the catastrophic history of the Jews during this century. I was born in 1932 and grew up in an assimilated household. My father was Jewish, my mother wasn't. My father was dismissed from his university post and had to wear the Jewish star. Until then, I knew nothing about Jews and the Jewish tradition. My Jewish films are a way of confronting my Jewish past and of working through my own guilt feelings. The guilt of a half-Jew. Why was I spared while so many perished? Non-Jews killed Jews.

Philo Bregstein graduated in law, wrote novels, and at the age of thirty began studying film, enrolling at the Centro Sperimentale Cinematografia in Rome.

"As for making Jewish films," Bregstein continued, "for me the turning point came when I read *The Destruction of the Dutch Jews*[1] by Jacques Presser. As noted earlier, *Destruction* took Holland by storm.

Presser worked on *The Destruction of the Dutch Jews* for fifteen years, 1950–1965. In it, he accused the Dutch of collaborating with the Hitler regime in Holland and complicity in the murder of Dutch Jewry. The war exposed the almost total lack of concern on the part of the Dutch towards the Jews, which came as a great blow to Presser. He was shattered and struggled with these experiences for the rest of his life.

Presser died in 1970, a week before *The Past That Lives* aired on Dutch TV. The film, which he himself narrated, became his testament, an intensely personal statement about the upheavals he lived through and the mark they left on him as a survivor and a historian. The experience of the war drove him back to his Jewish roots. It made a tremendous impression on me, shook me up completely, triggering a personal awakening which led me to reexamine my own past, a *recherche du temps perdu*. I just had to know what happened in the Nazi era.

Born at the end of the nineteenth century, the son of a poor diamond worker, Presser grew up in Amsterdam's Jewish ghetto, which was only a ghetto in the sense that most Jews happened to live in this part of Amsterdam. Early on Presser became fascinated with the Renaissance and Dutch socialism, a movement in which Jews

1. See Chapter V, fn. 26.

played a prominent role. Channeling Swiss cultural historian Jacob Burckhardt, he credited the Renaissance with having rediscovered the individual and believed socialism would uplift the working class and make short work of antisemitism. He regarded Holland as a country which allowed Jews to assimilate without giving up their Jewishness. He himself felt completely assimilated as a Dutchman in Dutch society. He loved German culture. Then came the war.

Within days of the German invasion, Presser and his wife, Dé (Debora), sought to escape to England via the port city of Ijmuiden. The roads were jammed, blocking their exodus. Back home in Amsterdam, they slit their wrists, backtracked, and went on with their lives as best as they could. They registered as Jews, sewed the Jewish star on their clothing, had their identity cards stamped with a J, and respected the 8:00 P.M. curfew for Jews. On Thursday, March 18, 1943, however, en route to celebrate her mother's birthday (her parents were in hiding in the countryside), Dé was caught after 8:00 with a fake I.D., arrested, interned in Westerbork, and gassed in Sobibor eight days later. She was 29. Jacques went into hiding the following May and did not resurface until the end of the war.[2]

---

2. In hiding, Presser wrote *Homo submersus: Een roman uit de onderduik,* a

2. Breaking Point

In 1956, Presser completed the novella *De Nacht der Girondijnen* (Night of the Girondins).[3] Presser's novella was the winning entry in an annual competition designed to promote reading in the Netherlands. Between March 30 and April 6, 1957, dubbed The Week of the Book, customers who spent at least 4.50 guilders at a bookstore could bag the novella free of charge. That same year Presser, the now 58-year-old Professor of History at the University of Amsterdam, garnered the Netherlands' Lucy B. and C.W. van der Hoogt Prize, the same prize awarded ten years earlier to Bert Voeten, half his age. Like Voeten's "diary," *Nacht*'s setting was the war. "A moving and yet strictly controlled power of expression," declared the judges.

The foreword by the selection commission spelled out the novella's theme:

> The novella has the drama of Westerbork, the transit camp from which the transports left for the German death camps, as its subject. Life in the camp, the prospect of the inevitable weekly transports that governed every action and relationship, and the role of the Jewish police force, which played such a tragic role in the cynical German system of dehumanization, is rendered with razor-sharp acuity.

The foreword further observed that the jury debated whether the novella's subject matter wasn't too bleak in light of the Book of the Week's mandate, resolving, ultimately, that it was not, for "[t]he novel treats a drama that confronts our entire nation."

That drama was the destruction of Dutch Jewry, a subject Presser spent fifteen years deconstructing, as noted by Bregstein. It wasn't

---

novel in the form of a diary. (Homo submersus: a novel written in hiding) (Amsterdam: Uitgeverij Boom, 2010).

3. *De nacht der Girondijnen* (Uitgever: Vereeniging ter bevordering van de belangen des boekhandels, 1957). The novella was translated into English as *Breaking Point* (Cleveland/New York: The World Publishing Company, 1958). Girondins: the liberal faction in the French Revolution, first victims of the Reign of Terror.

until he'd gotten the novella out of his system, Presser said, that he was able to start working on *Destruction*.[4]

The story runs as follows: Westerbork inmate Jacques Suasso Henriques, the novella's protagonist, is confined to the camp's Punishment Barrack. Barrack 67 held prisoners who had run afoul of the system, flouting one regulation or another. A Jew, say, caught in the act of escaping or caught afterwards; Jews betrayed in hiding, like the Franks in Amsterdam; getting on the wrong side of the commandant; going in public without the Jewish star, breaking curfew, possessing a fake identity card, as in Dé's case, etc. Punitive cases led off the weekly, and sometimes twice-weekly, deportation lists.

Suasso:

> A week has seven days. That week governs our lives. It starts and ends on Tuesday morning the minute the train leaves.... The train is the devil, a dragon from an evil myth, exuding enormous power as it emerges from the darkness with his dim headlights and shrill whistle screeching its triumph over us, slowly gliding, clank-clanking alongside the platform, hissing, steaming... And then it stops, splitting the camp in two, as though conjured from hell.

Jacques Suasso Henriques, a teacher at a Jews-only school, wound up in Westerbork through betrayal. As a so-called Portuguese Jew,[5] Suasso was exempted from deportation – until further notice. George Cohn came to the rescue. Cohn was a former student whose father, Siegfried Israël Cohn, a German Jew, served as the transit camp's Chief Administrator and Commandant Kurt Schaufinger's right-hand man. Cohn puts his cards on the table: every Jew, however useful to the commandant and crucial to the camp's operation, will one day be deported. "What can I, what can we do here? A ship with a thousand passengers has run a leak, and no one pays attention to our SOS signals. And there's room in the boats for fifty? One must be hard as nails."

The best he can do for Suasso, Cohn says, is to make sure that he'll be among the last to be deported.

---

4. Bregstein, *Gesprekken*, 121.
5. See Chapter IV.

Suasso's assignment is with the Westerbork's *Ordedienst* (O.D.), the camp's universally despised (Jewish) police force. As such, Suasso plays a major role in the "evacuation" of a Jewish mental institution, Amsterdam's Institute of the Blind, and a Jewish orphanage. An added duty is to report those plotting to escape.

A point of light on the "dreary plain" that is Westerbork is Jeremia Hirsch, a thirty-three-year-old teacher of religion; Suasso calls him "rebbe." Only Jeremia can make him laugh and yet engage him in a profoundly serious and deep conversation. As well, the "rebbe" helps Suasso recapture his Jewish and human roots. *Homo homini homo.*[6] The rebbe has a wife named Lea and two young children.

The week before landing in the Punishment Barrack, Suasso read out the list with the names of those earmarked for deportation in Barrack 57.[7] Jeremia Hirsch and his family were on it. "I helped him pack his rucksack; he consoled me. Jeremia, my friend, my brother." The train stood by, panting to take on its load. Hirsch carried a small, black book in one of his hands. On the platform, he tripped and dropped it. As he bent down with some difficulty owing to the weight of his backpack to retrieve it, Chief Administrator Cohn kicked it to the side, dragged Hirsch towards the train, and gave him a bloody nose to boot while Commandant Schaufinger looked on and smirked. "And then it happened, more quickly than I can relate it: I lunged at Cohn, hit him in the face as hard as I could, picked up the little book and returned it to the rebbe." About to enter the cattle car, the rebbe placed his hands on Suasso's head and blessed him. On Cohn's orders, the O.D. pounced on Jacques, hauling him off to the Punishment Barrack, accompanied by kicks and blows.

It is in Barrack 67, awaiting deportation, that Suasso writes up his story where he encounters Dé, a young woman with a scar on her wrist from an aborted suicide, whom he had known casually in the past.

And so now I've completed it. Even Dé was able to read it before it leaves the barrack…. The balance has been drawn up and there is

---

6. The novella's epigraph: homo homini homo – human to human.
7. Barrack 57 was my family's "home" in Westerbork.

a grand total, for better or for worse. She sat there for a long time, staring on front of her. At last, she came over to me and stroked my hair. . . . She takes it in stride. She's very brave, but also worried that her husband will get caught because of her. While she sews a button on my coat, I tell her to take heart.

'Say something, Dé, please!' She smiles. 'Tomorrow, when we're in the train. I am still processing everything, there are so terribly many questions. For example: why did you strike Cohn and not Schaufinger? No, don't try to explain. Tomorrow, in the train. In the train to Sobibor. In any case, from now on I'll give you your real name back: Jacob.'

For those in the know, guessing who's who is child's play. Siegfried Israël Cohn is Westerbork's Chief Administrator Kurt Schlesinger, in the camp known as the "Jewish SS man"; Commandant Kurt Schaufinger is Commandant Albert Konrad Gemmeker, and Dé, of course is Presser's wife. In Presser's telling, the compilation of the weekly deportation list, presided over by the commandant and the Jewish camp leadership, is a masterly account of the camp's lethal pecking order, a pitiless selection preapproved for destruction: the punitive cases, the sick, the old, and the infirm, families with small children, mothers and their six-week-old babies[8]; new arrivals without exemptions, as well as inmates whose stay of execution had lapsed.

Presser wrote about Westerbork in the first person, as though he were there. Like most Dutch Jews, he'd endured his own hell and poured a good deal of himself into the novella. *Breaking Point*, to use the title of the English translation, is fiction – or is it? Presser himself isn't so sure. Except for some small details, everything in the novella, Presser insisted, is "completely historical. . . . I wrote that novella in a kind of a trance."[9]

---

8. It will be recalled that my family's camp card indicates that the exemption based on my mother's pregnancy and six weeks "maternity leave" had expired, freeing us up for deportation. See Chapter 1, fn 1.

9. Bregstein, *Gesprekken*, 121.

3. *The Destruction of the Dutch Jews*

It isn't much of a stretch to characterize both the 65-page *Breaking Point* and the two-volume, 1,000-page *The Destruction of the Dutch Jews* as "egodocuments," a term Presser is credited with having coined. In egodocuments – "autobiographical writing, such as memoirs, diaries, letters and travel accounts – the I, the writer, is continuously present in the text as the writing and describing subject," an appreciation of history in which "the individual, 'the irreplaceable persona,' plays the central role and constitutes the "chief *source* of historical knowledge,"[10] though not, Presser adds emphatically, the "writing of history itself."[11] On the other hand, Presser didn't think there was all that much to choose between literature (*belles lettres*) and history proper. For his part, the dividing line was never clear-cut.

The book, writes Presser in "To the Reader," was commissioned by the Netherlands Institute for War Documentation in January 1950.

> I considered it my duty to speak up for all those thousands doomed to eternal silence, whose last cries of despair went unheard, and whose ashes no one was allowed to gather.… One thing became clear to me in the process of writing this book: no single Jew who lived through that period can think dispassionately about the events here recorded.… Nor can the writer, who himself was one of them, pretend to have achieved an Olympian objectivity. His choice was to write or remain silent. He chose to write; his heart demanded it.[12]

Destruction is "the story of murder on a scale never known before," Presser elaborates elsewhere.

> The murderers were Germans, their victims Jews – in the Netherlands they added up to a hundred thousand, less than 2 per cent of the total of those killed by the Nazis in the course of their fi-

---

10. As defined by the Center for the Study of Egodocuments and History. http://www.egodocument.net/egodocument/ (accessed April 13, 2023).
11. Bregstein, *Gesprekken*, 126.
12. Presser, *Destruction*, xiii-xiv.

nal solution of the Jewish problem. In this process, Dutch Jewry was put outside the law, isolated, robbed of all its possessions, deported, and cut down with near-scientific precision: city people, country-folk, believers, and free-thinkers, the healthy and the sick, old and young, Dutchmen and foreigners, men, women, and children. All this was done with great haste, with typical German thoroughness, and with due regard for the proper formalities. Many of the murderers were mere thugs and illiterates, but others were educated men with undeniable love of literature, art, and music; many were good family men, not without sensibility.[13]

As an "official history," *Destruction* had to be approved by the government. This took a while, for not everyone was on board. The head of the Institute for War Documentation, the historian Loe de Jong, balked at the chronology. Ben Sijes, Calmeyer's interviewer and labor historian, objected to the dearth of footnotes. The book finally came out in April 1965 and became an instant bestseller. From a first pressrun of 10,000 to 11,000, the totals gradually topped out at 130,000 to 140,000, meaning that 1.1% of the population bought it. This, Presser said, was the high note of his life, his "Sternstunde."[14]

Sales figures notwithstanding, *Destruction* was not without its critics.

Some found the book subjective, inadequately footnoted, containing figures that did not always add up, and short on context, specifically the absence of a prehistory of Dutch Jewry.... In short, the book unleashed an outburst of emotion. But after the dust had settled, we can say that *Destruction* constituted a milepost in Dutch historical writing. Although Presser was not the first author to write about the horrors of Jewish persecution, he was the first to reach a large segment of the Dutch population by virtue of his engagement, transparency, and accessibility. With this work

13. Ibid., 1.
14. The reference is to Stefan Zweig's *Sternstunde der Menschheit*, a compendium of decisive moments in history.

Presser achieved his goal: the dead have spoken and not a single person can now reduce them to silence.[15]

Presser said he wrote *Destruction* "with blood." Indeed, like "Suasso" on Westerbork's platform, the historian did not pull his punches. In contradistinction to the voluminous history of the Netherlands produced by Loe de Jong, parts of which necessarily covered the same ground, *Destruction* is a *de profundis*. Both historians were Jewish. Unlike Presser, De Jong made it to England in the nick of time and spent the war in London with the Dutch government in exile. The writing of *Destruction*, Presser told Bregstein, "shook him up a lot more than the actual experience."[16]

Presser reserved one of his most powerful blows for the Chairs of the Amsterdam Jewish Council, Professor David Cohen and diamond merchant Abraham Asscher. Called into existence by the occupier in February 1941, the Jewish Council was determined to save the most "valuable" Jews, inscribing themselves foremost in this classification. "First the men with the caps, and only then men with the hats."[17] The "two Presidents proved highly satisfactory to their masters," and so "it was certainly no accident "that they were allowed to remain at their posts, frequently urging Jews to obey the German regulations to the letter... But if the Presidents liked to see themselves as the captains of a sinking ship, they should have remembered the captain of the *Titanic* who did not take to the boats but perished in the waves." In May 1943, the Council was ordered to deliver 7,000 names for deportation. "The writer must put on record that among the 7,000 names, two were conspicuous by their absence: those of Asscher and Cohen."

Presser considered the page devoted to the Jewish Council and these two "upstanding, decent men" "the central page of the entire book," and the most painful to write.[18] His understanding of the task of the historian, he said, left him no choice but to indict the co-chairs.

---

15. Nico Markus, introduction to Jacques Presser's *Homo submersus*, 31.
16. *Gesprekken*, 94.
17. Presser, *Nacht*, 56.
18. Bregstein,*Gesprekken*, 125.

Having spent fifteen years sifting one document after another, it dawned on him that "one of the tasks of the historian, the individual who writes about people in the past, is to lend a voice to the dead. The dead must be allowed to speak, for if we prevent them from doing so, then they die twice."[19]

Abraham Asscher and Professor David Cohen were arrested in November 1947, charged with collaboration. The proceedings were dropped.

"More than once," Presser mused, "the writer has wondered where precisely the line between

> the historian and the jurist must be drawn, but though this question has weighed heavily upon him throughout his labors, he was unable to find a satisfactory answer. In theory it is, of course, possible to draw such a line, though we might add that this task is much easier for the jurist who, no doubt, can dig up some precedent in law to decide, for instance, whether or not the very foundation and continuance of the Jewish Council constituted collaboration with the enemy, and whether the claim made by apologists for the Jewish Council, that if they had not carried out various German orders, those orders would have been still more ruthlessly imposed, can be accepted as a valid defense. But clear as the issue may be to the jurist, it is anything but clear to the historian.[20]

But then, Presser proceeded, "[d]id not Dutch municipal officers collaborate in the registration of Jews and in placing the letter 'J' on Jewish identity cards? Did not virtually all officials sign

> the 'Aryan' declaration?[21] Did not the Dutch authorities collaborate in the dismissal of Jewish civil servants? Did not the Dutch Bench implement many of the German decrees. Did not the Department of Social Affairs, the municipalities and the District Labour Offices allow themselves to be used to draft Jews to the

---

19. The pages devoted to the Jewish Council, 264–277.
20. Presser, *Destruction*, 265.
21. Declaration testifying to "Aryan" descent by Dutch civil servants.

work-camps? Did not the Amsterdam municipality play an important part in herding Jews together? Did not the municipal transport system, the railways and the police, help in the deportations, and the gendarmerie in guarding Westerbork camp? Did the Dutch authorities refuse to collaborate in the confiscation of Jewish radios and bicycles, in depriving Jews of telephones? Did banks and clearing-houses refuse to hand over Jewish effects to Lippmann, Rosenthal & Company,[22] or did the Stock Exchange refuse to transfer Jewish shares?'[23]

4. Calmeyer, Weinreb, Israel

CALMEYER

Presser's take on Hans Georg Calmeyer left no room for doubt. "There is unanimous testimony that Calmeyer was highly intelligent, extremely conscientious, and utterly incorruptible…. There is little doubt that hundreds of Jews owe their lives to him, that it would have been a disaster if his place had been filled by a good Party man, and that he ran untold personal risks.[24] He described himself as "a typical lawyer and therefore inclined to believe the opposite of what I am told." Always looking for possible loopholes to save Jews. "The crux of his plea was that he found himself in a hopeless position, comparable to that of a doctor "in a lonely post, cut off from the outside world, and left with a mere 50 phials of medicine for the treatment of 5,000 critical cases.'"

Presser cites "a heart-rending appeal of a mother for her son ('an old, sick, nearly blind, poverty-stricken lonely mother, for her completely innocent, deserving boy') who asked Calmeyer to 'remember your own mother.'" Another petitioner used a different tack. "He told Calmeyer in no uncertain terms what he thought of his 'utterly indefensible decision'; we still have Calmeyer's reply – it says much

22. German looting bank, despite its Jewish-sounding name.
23. Presser, *Destruction*, 273–74.
24. For Calmeyer, see *Destruction*, 297–311.

for him that he answered the insulting letter, and did not report its writer to the authorities."[25]

> People have argued for and against Calmeyer's conduct. The writer of this work, for one, has not the slightest doubt that Calmeyer was skating on exceedingly thin ice, that he was working under duress and that, had he gone further than he did, he would, in fact, have jeopardized what little help he was able to give to the Jews. It is quite clear, for instance, that particularly after the beginning of the deportations, Calmeyer was inundated with so many obviously bogus applications that there was little he could do about them. Impossible cases crossed his desk, requiring king Solomon's proverbial wisdom to decide, had he been of that race.[26]

"What does seem clear," concludes Johannes Max van Ophuijsen, expatiating on the former Race Consultant's enduring sway, "is that both Presser in his *Destruction* and De Jong in his *Kingdom* evinced considerable empathy with the plight of a German fellow intellectual, a man of some culture and taste, whom they were confident they found sufficiently 'full of the milk of human kindness' to be able to nourish, however paradoxically, a sense of kinship with him."[27]

FRIEDRICH WEINREB

Like Calmeyer, Friedrich Weinreb claimed to have saved many a Jew from deportation and certain death at the risk of his own life. Writing in English for an American public Weinreb, a Dutch-Jewish economist of Polish origin, said that while the great majority of Dutch people were busily kowtowing to the German occupier, "[o]ne single Jew, Frederic Weinreb … decided to take action, without anybody's help, and evolved a plan so fantastic in scope and design, as will only be equaled by few other mystery plots in recent underground-history."

25. *Destruction*, 298–99.
26. Ibid., 299.
27. Johannes Max van Ophuijsen "'Indifferent Honest'? The Posthumous Charm of a Rassenreferent," *Osnabrücker Geschichtsblog*, September 27, 2022, http://hvos.hypotheses.org/7987 (accessed March 1, 2023).

On Tuesday, May 27, 1947, Weinreb appeared before the Special Court adjudicating "political delinquents." Meeting for the first time in public session, the Special Court heard testimony from witnesses who accused the former economist of having swindled large sums of money out of Jews by pretending he had a "list," approved by the German High command, which would enable Jews on it to emigrate to South America in exchange for foreign funds and German prisoners. There was not one but many lists, all of which eventually came to grief.[28] Weinreb himself went into hiding in February 1944.

Weinreb received a three-and-a-half-year prison sentence, less time served. In 1948, the Special Appeals Court revised the sentence upward to six years. "These courts concluded that Weinreb had used his lists to save himself and his family, to pay off the Nazis, and, to make a bundle in the process." After much back and forth between contending parties and interpretations, Weinreb was released in December 1948, after a successful appeal. Weinreb next published *Collaboration and Resistance* (1969) – three volumes, 1,800 pages – a complete index of his wartime exploits and indictment of Dutch collaboration. Clearly tired of clichés about life-saving pills and lifeboats, Weinreb invoked a burning building:

> I see a burning building, with the enemy carrying off all those who escape by the main entrance. I call out to the people in the building that the main entrance is elsewhere, and I lead them to a secret cellar. They think they are going to the main entrance and are grateful to me. Meanwhile I save them from the enemy. Yes, I lie and deceive them, but only to help then … If I had told them, I was taking them to the cellar no one would have followed me.

Elsewhere he referred to himself as a dealer in soap bubbles. "I gave the people who came to me a soap bubble with which they could dream a little longer before they were taken away."[29]

---

28. Our family card in Westerbork indicates that we were briefly on one of those lists.

29. For Friedrich Weinreb, see Jacob Boas, *Boulevard des Misères*, Chapter 6, 129–150.

Much like Presser's *Destruction*, Weinreb's book caused a sensation. There were calls for his rehabilitation. It was at this point that the Netherlands Institute for War Documentation got into the act. *Het Weinreb Rapport* (The Weinreb Report), two massive, folio-sized volumes almost six years in the making, came out in 1976. The report concluded that Weinreb was "one of the most successful fantasts of the Second World War whose every action was governed by 'personal desire for power, money and sex!'"

By then, Presser had been dead for seven years. In Volume II of the Dutch original, thus in 1965, Presser mounted a spirited defense of the maligned "dealer in soap-bubbles," absolving him of wrongdoing. Citing from the 1948 sentence "that the rule of law does not allow individuals to decide the fate of others based on their own conviction and moral standards," Presser countered that such a ruling condemned *all* illegal work. "Name an illegal worker who doesn't decide about the life and fate of others based on confidence in their own capacity and moral standard?"[30] He deserved better than a "heavy punishment."[31] Presser felt that "the Jew Weinreb has become the

> scapegoat, paying for the failure of numerous non-Jews. He had to fail, and did fail, because they had failed.... If there had been no Jewish traitors, they had to be invented. The few tried after the war didn't meet the quota. And now here was a big fish that answered to the need. This historian has never concealed the fact that this is a hypothesis, a personal conviction, but has made it sufficiently clear that he believes it, that he is convinced of it.[32]

Weinreb came up in my conversation with Philo Bregstein as well. Presser told Bregstein that Weinreb had once visited him after 1965, saying that he had heard that the historian had changed his mind. "I then declared what I have always declared, namely that ... I haven't been convinced by anyone of the opposite while I am completely open to be convinced of it.... At the time I wrote that Weinreb became

30. Presser, *Ondergang*, Vol II, 107.
31. Ibid., 109.
32. Ibid., 110.

the scapegoat of the non-Jews. Today I would have written: Weinreb became the scapegoat of both non-Jews and Jews."[33]

In the 1969 abridged English-language edition of Presser's *Ondergang* (*Destruction*), there is no mention of Friedrich Weinreb whatsoever. His name and *res gestae* seem to have been deliberately scrubbed. It was Loe de Jong, Presser's supervisor and the editor of *The Weinreb Report* who oversaw the publication of the condensed version.

ISRAEL

"Presser was no Zionist," Bregstein declared toward the tail-end of our conversation.

> He was not anti-Zionist, mind you, he said so himself, but in the final footage of the film *The Past That Lives* he rues the fact that there was no Israel before the war, no place of their own Jews could go to. At the same time, he warned about a new genocide in Israel. He warned about it because he felt that you could not allow yourself not to think about it. At the time, the world was blind about Auschwitz. Better to be awake and aware of the danger than lull yourself to sleep and find the end is upon you. That lesson should be learned by Jews and non-Jews alike, for it is essential for the survival of humanity.

Presser's conversations with Bregstein took place two years after the Six-Day War of 1967, at the conclusion of which Israel occupied Gaza, the West Bank, the Gaza Strip, Old City of Jerusalem, the Sinai Peninsula, and the Golan Heights. Even so, Presser considered Israel a "besieged" state. "One can never," he told Bregstein, "measure a besieged state with the same standards as other states.

> If Israel was to suffer a devastating defeat at the hands of the Arabs, the world will see a second genocide. I can say that this is something that I can't let go off lately. I say 'the world.' Because it isn't a problem of the poor Palestinians. If these people consider themselves to have been driven from their home, then I would say:

---

33. Bregstein, *Gesprekken*, 136.

who better to sympathize than the Jews who know what it means to be uprooted, to be exiled. To my mind, the Palestinians are nothing more than pawns on a chessboard. It is the problem of those who in 1940–45 and before defaulted. And should they default once more, I wonder – and I hope I am not too bleak – Israel has no choice but to do whatever it takes to guarantee its survival. This is not a matter for the Arabs and Palestinians, this is a matter for the world to resolve. The world will decide, and I'm not all that optimistic as regards that decision. For as long the world is still absent, I cannot blame the Jews for trying with all their might to prevent a genocide.[34]

5. Vindicating History

Reviewing the years 1939–1959, Presser approvingly cited Marc Bloch's views on teaching and studying history.

> My point of departure is the elusive nature of history, art *and* scholarship, knowledge, *and* pleasure. In a way that is difficult to identify, almost impossible to pin down, it contributes to the formation of the human personality, even among those who reject it, or think they can reject it. Of Winston Churchill it was once said: 'His sense of history never failed.' Sense of history: it is no coincidence that in times of danger...a society turns to history. I don't intend to be wiser than Goethe with his oft-quoted *Das Beste, was wir von der Geschichte haben, ist der Enthusiasmus den sie erregt* – 'The best thing about history is that it arouses our enthusiasm.' Permit me to put my own gloss on this utterance and once more invoke the 'sense of history' as the most important thing to be gained from a 'useless' but indispensable subject.[35]

34. Ibid., 128–130.
35. J. Presser, "Na twintig jaar: Onpedagogische bespiegelingen over een geschiedenisles" (Twenty years later: unpedagogical reflections on a history lesson), in *Schrijfsels en schrifturen* (Scribbles and writings) (Amsterdam: Moussault's Uitgeverij, 1961), 123–137. Here 135–36. The quotation is from Bloch's *Apologie pour l'histoire*.

Paul Valéry compared historians to card-readers. Not surprising for someone who considered history "the most dangerous product evolved from the chemistry of the intellect," observed Presser in the same collection that produced the Goethe citation. "Can we," Presser proceeded, "deduce an answer from the way in which we view the past to the question of how we will view our own time a few centuries from now?" And concludes, demonstrating the seemingly unshakeable belief in unlimited progress of a bygone century, that the twentieth does not come off too shabby, gas chambers, the atom bomb, and germ warfare notwithstanding. To be sure, we could have done more, Presser acknowledges, "but centuries from now might historians not only look upon our current species with irony and pity, but also with reverence and admiration for what we have accomplished?"[36]

* * *

* *

*

---

36. "Mijmeringen over een Gouden Eeuw" (Musing about a Golden Century"), in *Schrijfsels en schrifturen*, 93–100. Here 94 and 99. The century is Holland's seventeenth, the century of "Rembrandt, Grotius, and Spinoza."

Bibliography

Aalders, Gerard. *Roof: De ontvreemding van joods bezit tijdens de Tweede Wereldoorlog*. Den Haag. SdU Uitgevers, 1999.

Aarts, Jan, Hoogewoud, F.J., en Kooyman, Chris. *Ex libris in exil: duits-joodse vluchtelingen in Nederland 1933–1940*. Amsterdam: De Buitenkant, volume 14, No. 2/3/2011.

Aarts, Jan & Kooyman, Chris. With a contribution by Hoogewoud. F.J. *Dit is mijn boek: Joodse exlibriscultuur in Nederland*. Amsterdam: De Buitenkant, 2017.

Aufsätze aus der Kampfzeit (München: Franz Eher Nachfolger, 1935). *Der Angriff*, July 30, 1928. https://ghdi.ghi-dc.org/docpage.cfm ?docpage_id=5905&language=german.

Baartse, Dirk. "Kultuurkamergeleerde." In *De God van Nederland ziet alles!* January-March 2014, No. 10, 38–39.

Baltschev, Bettina. *Hel en Paradijs: Amsterdam en de Duitse exilliteratuur*. Trans. Mark Wildschut. Amsterdam: Antwerpen, Querido, 2017.

Bloch, Marc. *The Historian's Craft*. Trans. from the French (*Apologie pour l'histoire*) by Peter Putnam. New York, Vintage Books, 1953.

Boas, Jacob, *Boulevard des Misères: The Story of Transit Camp Westerbork* (Hamden Connecticut, Archon Books, 1985).

———. *We Are Witnesses: Five Diaries of Teenagers Who Died in the Holocaust*. New York: Square Fish/Macmillan, 2009.

Braak, Menno ter. *Cultural Criticism in the Netherlands, 1933–1940: The Newspaper Columns of Menno ter Braak*. Introduced. Introduced, edited and translated by Jacob Boas. Leiden/Boston: Brill/Rodopi, 2020.

————"Georg Hermann 'Plaudert.'" *Het Vaderland*, March 16, 1937.

Brakmann, Thomas. "Der Fall Calmeyer ('Het geval Calmeyer') – eine Zusammenfassung." https://hvos.hypotheses.org/5180.

Bregstein, Philo. *Gesprekken met Jacques Presser*. Amsterdam: Polak & Van Gennep Uitgeversmaatschappij NV, 1971.

Bregstein, Philo and Bloemgarten, Salvador. *Herinnering aan Joods Amsterdam*. Amsterdam: Uitgeverij De Bezige Bij, 1978.

Broch, Hermann. *The Sleepwalkers*, trans. Willa and Edwin Muir. San Francisco: North Point Press, 1985.

Cixous, Hélène. *Osnabrück Station to Jerusalem: A Memoir*. Transl. Peggy Kamuf. New York: Fordham University Press, 2020.

Cixous, Hélène. *Well-Kept Ruins*. Trans. Beverley Bie Brahic. London, New York, Calcutta: Seagull Books, 2022.

Craig-Sharples, John. *Georg Hermann: A Writer's Life*. Cambridge: Legenda, 2019.

Cultural Plunder by the Einsatzstab Reichsleiter Rosenberg. https://www.errproject.org./guide.php.

Diggelen, Els van and Edelstein, Alfred. "Femmas lijdensweg sinds 1943 zaait anno 2020 paniek." https://www.ewmagazine.nl/opinie/achtergrond/2020/10/femmas-lijdensweg-sinds-1943-zaait-anno-2020-paniek-779735/?utm_referrer=https%3A%2F%2Fduckduckgo.com%2F.

Franz Josef Müller im Gespräch mit Christoph Lindenmeyer (2003). https://www.br.de/fernsehen/ard-alpha/sendungen/alpha-forum/franz-josef-mueller-gespraech100.html.

Goldstein, Moritz. "German Jewry's Dilemma. The Story of Provocative Essay." *Year Book of the Leo Baeck Institute*, Volume 2, Issue 1, January 1957.

Heijden. Chris van der. *Grijs verleden: Nederland en de Tweede Wereldoorlog*. Amsterdam/Antwerpen: Uitgeverij Contact, 2001.

Himmler, Heinrich. The Complete Text of the Poznan Speech. https://phdn.org/archives/holocaust-history.org/himmler-poznan/speech-text.shtml.

Horváth, Ödön von. *Jugend ohne Gott*. www.literaturdownload.at/Horvath.html.

Interview mit Herrn Franz Müller (Weiße-Rose-Stiftung, 29.09.2011). https://edisciplinas.usp.br/pluginfile.php/256444/course /section/78106/anotacoes-mueller.pdf.

Jaren '40–'45, De. Rijksinstituut voor oorlogsdocumentatie (Netherlands Institute for War Documentation), 1961.

joodsmonument.nl

Junk, Peter and Sellmeyer, Martina. *Stationen auf dem Weg nach Auschwitz: Entrechtung, Vertreibung, Vernichtung, Juden in Osnabrück 1900–1945. Ein Gedenkbuch.* Osnabrück: Rach Verlag Bramsche, 1988.

Ketelaar, Eric. "Unravelling the Mesh: The ERR Survey as a Finding Aid." https://www.obs-traffic.museum/sites/default/files /ressources/files/Ketelaar_Unravelling_the_Mesh.pdf.

Lang, Wally de. *De razzia's van 22 en 23 februari 1941 in Amsterdam: het lot van 389 Joodse mannen.* Amsterdam/Antwerpen: Atlas Contact, 2021.

Lipshiz, Canaan. "Did Hans Calmeyer Send a Jewish Woman to Auschwitz?" *The Jerusalem Post*, May 7, 2020. https://www.jpost .com/diaspora/antisemitism/did-hans-calmeyer-send-a-jewish -woman-to-auschwitz-627181.

Luijters, Guus. *In Memoriam: De gedeporteerde en vermoorde Joodse, Roma en Sinti kinderen 1942.* Amsterdam: Nieuw Amsterdam Uitgevers, 2012.

———"Rapenburg 26-huis, Amsterdam." In *Joodse huizen 5: verhalen over vooroorlogse bewoners* (https://gibbonuitgeefagentschap.nl/, 2019, 143–55.

Meijer, Ischa. *De interviewer en de schrijvers.* https://www.dbnl.org /tekst/meij012inte04_01/meij012inte04_01_0017.php.

Middelberg, Mathias M. "Calmeyer war ein Menschenretter." *Osnabrücker Geschichtsblog*, June 9, 2020. https://hvos.hypotheses .org/5194.

Minco, Marga. *Verzamelde verhalen: 1951–1981.* Amsterdam: Uitgeverij Bert Bakker, 1982.

Nussbaum, Laureen. "A Sampling of Georg Hermann's 'Letters about German Literature.'" *Algemeen Handelsblad* 1921–1926." In *Georg*

Hermann: *Deutsch-jüdischer Schriftsteller und Journalist, 1871–1943.* Halle and Tübingen: Max Niemeyer Verlag, 2004.

———"Hans Calmeyer ist 'ein stiller Held,'" June 16, 2020, https://hvos.hypotheses.org/5226.

———with Kirtley, Karen. *Shedding Our Stars: The Story of Hans Calmeyer and How He Saved Thousands of Families Like Mine.* Berkeley, California: She Writes Press, 2019.

Ophuijsen, Johannes Max van. "'Indifferent Honest'? The Posthumous Charm of a Rassenreferent," *Osnabrücker Geschichtsblog,* September 27, 2022. http://hvos.hypotheses.org/7987.

Osnabrücker Geschichtsblog.

Peel, Peter. "The Life and Death of Alfred Rosenberg." http://www.renegadetribune.com/the-life-and-death-of-alfred-rosenberg/.

Presser, Jacob. *Ondergang: De vervolging en verdelging van het Nederlandse Jodendom 1940–1945* ('S-Gravenhage: Staatsuitgeverij, 1965. Two volumes. *The Destruction of the Dutch Jews.* Trans. Arnold Pomerans. New York, E.P. Dutton, Inc., 1969.

———De nacht der Girondijnen. Vereeniging ter bevordering van de belangen des boekhandels, 1957.

———*Schrijfsels en schrifturen.* Amsterdam: Moussault's Uitgeverij, 1961.

Rebel, mijn hart: kunstenaars 1940–45. Zwolle: Uitgeverij Waanders, 1995.

Remak, Joachim, ed., The Nazi Years: A Documentary History. Prospect Heights, Illinois: Waveland Press, 1990.

Renders, Hans. "Adriaan Venema: Het dagboek. Een roman over '40–'45." NRC Handelsblad, March 23, 1993.

Romijn, Peter. *Der lange Krieg der Niederlande: Besatzung, Gewalt und Neuorientierung in den vierziger Jahren.* Göttingen: Wallstein Verlag, 2017.

Salamanderboekˆ, Het. Amsterdam: N.V. EM Querido Uitgeversmaatschappij, 1938.

Sanders, Joop. *Bittergeld: De restitutie van geroofde Joodse oorlogstegoeden.* Nederland: Verbum en Joop Sanders, 2022.

Scherzer, Herbert. "Kabarett in Amsterdam während des Zweiten Weltkriegs." *Aufbau,* August 28, 1987.

Schneberg, Willa. *Kaddish For Felix Nussbaum (1904–1944)*.

Stevens, Christa. LIEJ – Littérature et Judéité. "'Les plis noir de la grande tragedie': sur Gare d'Osnabrück à Jerusalem d'Hélène Cixous." https://liej.hypotheses.org/christa-stevens.

Stigter, Bianca. *Atlas van een bezette stad: Amsterdam, 1940–1945*. Amsterdam: Atlas Contact, 2019.

Thelen, Albert Vigoleis. "Georg Hermann scheitert," *Het Vaderland*, July 22, 1934.

———"Romane von Georg Hermann und Hermann Kesten. Ein Buch über Struensee. *Die Literatur in der Fremde: Literaturkritiken*. Ed., trans. and with a foreword by Erhard Louven (Bonn: Weidle, 1966).

Tilman, Westphalen. "Die Würde des Menschen ist unantastbar." In Erich Maria Remarque, *Der Funke Leben*. Köln: Kiepenheuer & Witsch, 1998.

Timms, Edward. *Karl Kraus, Apocalyptic Satirist: The Post-War Crisis and the Rise of the Swastika*. New Haven and London: Yale University Press, 2005.

Venema, Adriaan. *Schrijvers, uitgevers en hun collaboratie*, 1: het system. Amsterdam: Arbeiderspers, 1988.

———*Verleden tijd: Memoires*. Amsterdam: Uitgeverij Balans, 1994.

Wagt, Wim de. *Vijfhonderd meter namen: De Holocaust en de pijn van de herinnering*. Amsterdam: Boom, 2021.

White Rose Pamphlets (English) at http://www.historyisaweapon .com/defcon1/whiterose.html.

White Rose sentencing transcripts. https://libcom.org/library/white -rose-sentencing-transcripts.

Archives

FelixArchief, Antwerpen.

National Archives. Holocaust International Resources. https://www
.archives.gov/research/holocaust/international-resources/nara
/err.

https://invenio.bundesarchiv.de/invenio/main.xhtml.

Niedersächsisches Landesarchive

NIOD. Institute for war, holocaust and genocide studies. Archief
93a, Einsatzstab Rosenberg inv. No. 63. https://www.archieven.nl
/nl/zoeken?miadt=298&mizig=210&miview=inv2&milang=nl&
micols=1&micode=093a&mizk_alle=093a&mip2=63.

Stadsarchief Amsterdam. https://www.amsterdam.nl/stadsarchief/

https://www.amsterdam.nl/stadsarchief/agenda/
razzia-22–23-februari-1941/

Westerbork Archives

Picture credits

Family camp card (Westerbork Archive)
Neck kiss (still from *Jud Süss*)
Himmler (German Federal Archive)
Raid on Jewish Quarter (Netherlands State Institute for War Documentation; NIOD)
Dagloonder Family Card (Stadsarchief Amsterdam)
Inventory Register (NIOD, Archief 93a)
Alfred Rosenberg (United States Army Signal Corps)
Georg Hermann Borchardt (Jewish Museum, Berlin)
Jettchen Gebert (filmportal.de)
Jekkerstraat (joodsamsterdam.nl)
Georg Borchardt's Family Card (Stadsarchief Amsterdam)
Georg Borchardt's Jewish Council Card (Westerbork Archive)
Hans and Sophie Scholl with Christoph Probst (haus-des-errinerns-mainz)
Villa Schlikker (Osnabrücker Geschichtsblog)
4J – four Jewish grandparents (Screen shot *Het raadsel van Femma*)
Hans Georg Calmeyer (www.dedokwerker.nl/hans_calmeyer.html)
Jonas Haus (Hélène Cixous, *Well-Kept Ruins*)
Application form for one person of full or part Jewish blood (Osnabrücker Geschichtsblog)
Felix Nussbaum. Self Portrait with Jewish Identity Card (felix-nussbaum-haus, Osnabrück).
Adriaan Venema (*VerledenTijd: Memoires*)
Treedt niet toe tot de Gilden! (*Rebel, mijn hart: kunstenaars 1940–45*)
Wedding Day (*Gesprekken met Jacques Presser*)